IRRESISTIBLE
to
God

STEVE
GALLAGHER

ACKNOWLEDGEMENTS

Special thanks to Brad Furges and Linus Minsk for their invaluable contributions to this book.

DEDICATION

To Jeff and Rose Colon, irresistible saints who have
humbled themselves before God and live their lives to
serve the needs of others.

TABLE OF CONTENTS

INTRODUCTION

THERE HAVE BEEN ONLY A HANDFUL OF occurrences in history when the veil of darkness enshrouding the Almighty has become thin enough for mortals to get a glimpse of the awe-inspiring reality of His overwhelming presence.

For example, this happened when the Israelites were given the Ten Commandments. With utmost solemnity, Moses had warned them to "prepare to meet thy God." Thus, nearly three million Hebrew men, women and children stood in the natural rock amphitheater at the base of Mount Sinai nervously gazing up at its craggy heights. Surrounding them along the hillsides were arrayed myriads of invisible "chariots of God." (Psalm 68:17)

Suddenly, the tranquil setting was disrupted by a whirlwind of activity as the great and dreadful Jehovah descended upon the mountaintop. Lightening and thunderbolts lit up the blackened sky and a deafening trumpet sound came forth. (Hebrews 12:18-19) "The mountain burned with fire to the very heart of the heavens: darkness, cloud and thick gloom." (Deuteronomy 4:11) The people screamed and cowered in paralyzing fear, pleading with Moses to stand between them and the terrible God of Sinai. "Go down, warn the people," Jehovah told Moses, "lest they break through to the Lord to gaze, and many of them perish." (Exodus 19:21)

Another occasion when man was able to "see" God occurred nearly a thousand years later when the prophet Isaiah "in the year of King Uzziah's death," saw this terrifying Being sitting on His throne, with mighty seraphim flying around Him crying, "Holy, Holy, Holy, is the Lord of hosts, the whole earth is full of His glory. And the foundations of the thresholds trembled at the voice of him who called out, while the temple was filling with smoke." (Isaiah 6:1-4)

Later, Isaiah heard the Almighty boom out, "Heaven is My throne, and the earth is My footstool. Where then is a house you could build for Me? And where is a place that I may rest?" (Isaiah 66:1-2) Undoubtedly this left him "full of fear and trembling" as happened to Moses. (Hebrews 12:21) But in a holy, yet paradoxical, manner this fearsome Being, seems to soften His countenance and finishes His statement with a wistful, longing tone in His voice: "But to this one I will look, to him who is humble and contrite of spirit, and who trembles at My word." (Isaiah 66:2)

What an astonishing statement! God looking to a human being! The Hebrew word for "look" (*nabat*) has a much stronger connotation than its English counterpart. It means to intently gaze upon an object with respect and adoration. Imagine this omnipotent God, whose return to earth will cause the sun to go black, the stars to fall from the sky, and the heavens to shake, (Matthew 24:29) regarding and esteeming dust! Such truth is simply incomprehensible, but nonetheless, it is recorded in the Holy Scripture.

Isaiah was not the only one to get such a revelation about the Lord. Several centuries before, David had gotten a sight of Him and penned these words: "For though the Lord is exalted, yet He regards the lowly; but the haughty He knows from afar." (Psalm 138:6) This verse reiterates the words in Isaiah 66 but adds a contrasting truth. While He draws near to the humble, He naturally repels—is set against—the prideful. Thus, close contact or true fellowship between the Almighty and the proud in heart is impossible.

These statements reflect a spiritual law—much like sowing and reaping—that holds true for both believers and nonbelievers alike. Clearly, high-minded people who reduce the Lord to human levels are on extremely dangerous ground, for "God opposes the proud." (James 4:4)

Unfortunately, most believers' perspective of pride is so superficial that it makes them oblivious to its presence in their own lives. They can easily identify it in swaggering Hollywood actors, snooty rich people, egotistical sports stars, or even a loud-mouthed co-worker. But ask them if *they* struggle with being prideful and most likely denial will kick in right away. "Oh, no! Not me!" What contemporary pastor has ever had an anxious church member come into his office lamenting over his struggles with pride?

Whether or not we recognize its odious presence, pride lurks within every human heart. It is a corrosive agent that permeates our fallen nature and eats away at one's soul if left undetected. Indeed, there is much within the human heart that exalts itself against God. (II Corinthians 10:5)

This book is a road map that shows the arduous but rewarding way out of the pit of pride and into the green pastures of humility. Before one can approach the blessed regions of lowliness, he must first courageously take a personal inventory of his life. He must be willing to have every dimension of pride exposed and dealt with in order to discover his proper position before a holy God.

As difficult and painful as it may be at times, such a path is the only way into the blessings of the Lord. It is the pilgrimage every godly saint has trekked. It is only when you honestly come to grips with the pride in your own life that you are ready to examine the subject of humility. Hence, this book is divided into two parts: *God Resists the Proud* (Part I) and *Irresistible to God* (Part II).

❧

"To this one I will look," Jehovah declared, "to him who is humble and contrite of spirit, and who trembles at My word." This is the person who makes himself *Irresistible to God!*

PART ONE
GOD RESISTS THE PROUD

"There is hardly a page of Scripture on which it is not clearly written that God resisteth the proud and giveth grace to the humble." [1]

Augustine

"Think, brother, what a sin it must be which has God for its opponent." [2]

Jerome

"How great is the evil of pride, that it rightly has no angel, nor other virtues opposed to it, but God Himself as its adversary!" [3]

John Cassian

one

THE NATURE AND REALM OF PRIDE

LTHOUGH ISAIAH'S MINISTRY EMERGED during the great reformation that came about through King Uzziah, he could not have been prepared for the tragedy his young eyes must have witnessed. The Lord struck down the old king with leprosy although he had done so much to overthrow evil in the land. What could this honorable man have done to provoke such a sudden execution of God's judgment?

Uzziah was only 16 years old when he succeeded his father as ruler over Judah. We are told the sincere young man "continued to seek God in the days of Zechariah... and as long as he sought the LORD, God prospered him." (II Chronicles 26:5) Indeed, it seemed that everything went right for him. He was able to restore rich commerce to the nation by building up the port of Elath. He subdued the Philistines, Ammonites and Arabians. He fortified the cities of Judah and assembled a mighty army. "His fame extended to the border of Egypt, for he became very strong." (II Chronicles 26:8)

Yet, at the height of his fame, prosperity and power, Uzziah became the victim of a human passion that has destroyed many lives:

But when he became strong, his heart was so proud that he acted corruptly, and he was unfaithful to the LORD his God, for he entered the temple of the LORD to burn incense on the altar of incense. Then Azariah the priest entered after him and with him eighty priests of the LORD, valiant men. And they opposed Uzziah the king and said to him, "It is not for you, Uzziah, to burn incense to the LORD, but for the priests, the sons of Aaron who are consecrated to burn incense. Get out of the sanctuary, for you have been unfaithful, and will have no honor from the LORD God."

But Uzziah, with a censer in his hand for burning incense, was enraged; and while he was enraged with the priests, the leprosy broke out on his forehead before the priests in the house of the LORD, beside the altar of incense. And Azariah the chief priest and all the priests looked at him, and behold, he was leprous on his forehead; and they hurried him out of there, and he himself also hastened to get out because the LORD had smitten him.

And King Uzziah was a leper to the day of his death; and he lived in a separate house, being a leper, for he was cut off from the house of the Lord. And Jotham his son was over the king's house judging the people of the land." (II Chronicles 26:16-21)

What could possibly have affected this respectable old king so much that he would act "corruptly" before his Lord? What kind of passion could incite him to behave so presumptuously with the sacred things of God? What would cause him to fall from the heights of human power and glory to being forced to live out the remainder of his life as a lonely old recluse in a leper's house? The answer to each of these questions is PRIDE.

The Bible certainly leaves no doubt as to what God's position is on pride. Solomon said that "a proud look" is an abomination to the Lord. (Proverbs 6:17) Isaiah wrote that when the Lord appears, "...the pride of man will be humbled, and the loftiness of men will be abased, and the Lord alone will be exalted in that day." (Isaiah 2:17) Jesus said, "...whoever exalts himself shall be humbled..." (Matthew 23:12) James said, "God is opposed to the proud..." (James 4:6) In Psalms, the Lord Himself said, "Whoever has haughty eyes and a proud heart, him will I not endure." (Psalm 101:5b NIV)

Unquestionably, pride is one of the most prominent subjects addressed in Scripture. The Bible uses at least 17 different words (and countless derivatives) to describe this spiritual disease.* However, no matter which term is used, there is almost always a connotation of height: something high, rising, exalted, or being lifted up. Thus, a proud person has a high estimation of himself and lifts himself above those around him. This concept of self-exaltation forms the basis for our working definition of pride: *Having an exaggerated sense of one's own importance and a selfish preoccupation with one's own rights.* It is the attitude that says, "I am more important than you and, if need be, I will promote my cause and protect my rights at your expense."

Pride is the governing principle of hell and the unredeemed world it influences. It causes strife in the home, the workplace, the political arena and yes, even the Christian

---

* For instance, in one sentence Jeremiah uses several terms to describe Moab: "We have heard of the pride (*ga'own*) of Moab—he is very proud (*ge'eh*)—of his haughtiness (*gobahh*), his pride (*ga'own*), his arrogance (*ga'own*) and his self-exaltation (*ruwm*)." (Jeremiah 48:29)

> **Pride is the governing principle of hell and the unredeemed world it influences.**

community. (Proverbs 13:10) Pride incites fierce competition amongst people in all facets of life.

It motivates girls to look sexy and attempt to out-dress each other as they vie for the position of "fairest of them all." Unwilling to be considered average, they do everything within their power to elevate themselves over their female rivals. High-minded men compete with each other over their physiques, prowess, abilities or possessions.

Pride fans the flames of lust that drive a sexual sinner straight down the spiral of degradation. A Don Juan feels a self-exalting exhilaration when he adds a new female to his conquests. A rapist feeds his monstrous ego by subjugating another. An exhibitionist becomes intoxicated with pride at the thought of a woman seeing his private parts. An adulteress swells up at the thought of stealing the amorous affections of a competitor's husband.

Pride is also behind much of the violence that plagues our world. An injured ego causes a man to kill his wife and her lover. Ethnic pride provokes escalating and inflammatory rhetoric between people groups which leads to war. Members of rival street gangs become involved in brawls and drive-by shootings in retaliation to previous attacks by their opponents. Barroom fights break out over petty disputes. Much unnecessary hostility occurs simply because people are trying to save face and gain one-upmanship. Without a doubt, pride has caused more problems, conflicts, suffering, and heartache on this earth than any other human passion.

There is a common denominator in each of these scenarios: people are either trying to exalt themselves at the expense of others or they are doing their utmost to protect themselves from others who would do so at *their* expense. Every bit of it reeks with the ugly and selfish attitude of "taking care of number one."

THE KINGDOM OF GOD

Long before God created man, a great rebellion occurred in heaven when the arch-angel Lucifer said in his heart, "I will ascend into heaven, I will exalt my throne above the stars of God: I will sit also upon the mount of the congregation, in the sides of the north: I will ascend above the heights of the clouds; I will be like the most High." (Isaiah 14:13-14) The same high-minded attitude that caused the king of pride to be cast out of heaven is the predominant mindset of this fallen world. As Scripture tells us, "The whole world lies in the power of the evil one." (I John 5:19) Satan now uses pride to provoke jealousy, anger, perversion and a litany of other vices common to man. Perhaps this motivated one minister to write:

Pride was the sin that turned Satan, a blessed angel, into a cursed devil. Satan knows better than anyone the damning power of pride. Is it any wonder, then, that he so often uses it to poison the saints? His design is made easier in that man's heart shows a natural fondness for it. [4]

> The same high-minded attitude that caused the king of pride to be cast out of heaven is the predominant mindset of this fallen world.

How utterly different is God's kingdom! His realm is governed by the innocent Lamb who allowed Himself to

21

be slaughtered *for the sake of others*. He is "meek and lowly in heart." (Matthew 11:29 KJV) The presiding mentality of those who faithfully follow Him is low-mindedness. Such individuals prefer the needs and wishes of others above their own.

It takes awhile for the new child of God to get used to this selfless thinking. As he attempts to live by the governing principles of the kingdom of heaven, he soon realizes that his old, selfish ways of thinking are still very much alive within him. Indeed, he still has a flesh nature that is permeated by pride. He finds himself torn between the self-promoting mentality of this world and the self-sacrificing values of God's kingdom.

A friend of mine—lamenting over his inability to gain ground against this venomous serpent—once likened his battle to throwing a firecracker at the side of a tall mountain. His effort might produce a temporary bang, but once the smoke clears, the mountain remains standing as formidable as ever. Charles Spurgeon shared my friend's bleak assessment of the battle when he wrote:

> Pride is so natural to fallen man that it springs up in his heart like weeds in a watered garden, or rushes by a flowing brook. It is an all pervading sin, and smothers all things like dust in the roads, or flour in the mill. Its every touch is evil. You may hunt down this fox, and think you have destroyed it, and lo! your very exultation is pride. None have more pride than those who dream that they have none. Pride is a sin with a thousand lives; it seems impossible to kill it. [5]

If pride is so pervasive and unconquerable in the human heart, why fight it at all? Surely God understands that it is a battle that cannot be won. Why enter a skirmish that one knows ahead of time he is sure to lose? Despite such gloomy appraisals, pride *must* be fought! The reason this battle is so urgent is because it is the nature of the devil himself. Every form that it takes within a person's character increases his resemblance to Satan himself. It is the fallen angel who provokes believers to promote, exalt, vaunt, and protect themselves at the expense of others. Much of pride's devilish workings are chalked up as being the norm—as if that alleviates a Christian's responsibility to overthrow its malignant influence within his life.

While it is true that there will always remain some trace of it, the alternative to allowing oneself to remain in a lofty, God-defying mindset is unthinkable to any sincere believer. Although a person may not totally eradicate all traces of pride within him, he can certainly make headway by acknowledging it and repenting whenever it rears its ugly head.

EVERYBODY'S PROBLEM

Different people have different sins that plague them. One man feels overwhelmed by sexual lust, while another doesn't feel a strong pull in that area. One person has a natural inclination to gossip; another has an explosive temper. Every human being alive has a propensity toward certain sins, while other vices hold no attraction. The variety is seemingly endless. However, *everybody* deals with pride because it is an inescapable part of the fallen nature.

Pride is so extremely subtle that many actually think they have little or none of it within them. The truth is that it has the ability to mask its presence within a person's heart. In fact, it is usually true that the more a person has, the less he is aware of it. Just like Spurgeon said, "None have more pride than those who dream that they have none."

Just as there are many forms and countless variations of sin, the same holds true of pride. Throughout the course of Part I, many of these different types of pride will be addressed, but for the sake of overview, let's take a look at an imaginary family. Bill Johnson is extremely smug over the fact that he built a successful business from scratch with nobody's help. His wife Nancy beams with self-satisfaction over their four children, talking about them to anybody who will listen. Seventeen-year-old Gwen has long, blond hair which she brushes endlessly in front of a mirror. Right behind her at sixteen is Josh, a linebacker on the football team known for his vicious tackles. Thirteen-year-old Ricky is the class comedian and always loves to be the center of attention. Suzy, who is extremely shy even for a twelve-year-old, has already built thick walls around her which nobody can penetrate. This describes your typical American family.

So what's the great crime in enjoying the admiration of others or in being a little protective? Pride—like any sin—is never satisfied and one ounce of pride is too much. Gwen's vanity might seem like a harmless teenage fancy, but left unchecked, it will eventually become an ugly monster of arrogance that will manifest itself in her life in many ways. If Suzy doesn't learn to make herself vulnerable to others, she will eventually close herself into a small world where there's no room for anybody else but herself.

In this family there is a common denominator between each person's predominant type of pride: the promotion and protection of almighty self. If they would ever become believers, they would discover self to be their biggest hindrance to becoming Christ-like and pride to be self's greatest sponsor.

The deeds, words, and thoughts that stem from one's pride are NOT "victimless crimes." When a person is prideful, he automatically lifts himself up at the expense of others.

For instance, Bill is oblivious to how his disdain for underlings has hurt their feelings many times. He privately glories in the fact that others fear him.

Nancy only wants to talk about *her* kids, and her noticeable lack of interest in others' children has often offended her friends and co-workers.

Gwen wants to be adored by all the boys and has little concern about other girls receiving attention. In fact, there have been times when less pretty girls have been crushed as she gloated over the attention she receives in front of them.

Josh's determination to win at any cost has made him a fierce competitor—even if it means seriously injuring another player. The look of searing pain on his victim's face is quickly forgotten as he triumphantly returns to the huddle.

Ricky is unconcerned that his daily comedy shows are a constant source of grief to his teacher who already has her hands full managing a rowdy bunch of adolescents.

Even bashful Suzy has often hurt others through her lack of responsiveness to their displays of affection. Her quiet determination to protect herself from being hurt, no matter what, takes precedence over their feelings.

GOD RESISTS THE PROUD

Before we go any further, it is time to face the spiritual reality that the Lord stands vehemently against every form of pride—whether in saint or sinner.* Peter admonished the Christians of the Early Church:

> You younger men, likewise, be subject to your elders; and all of you, clothe yourselves with humility toward one another, for God is opposed to (*resists* NKJV) the proud, but gives grace to the humble. Humble yourselves, therefore, under the mighty hand of God, that He may exalt you at the proper time, casting all your anxiety upon Him, because He cares for you. Be of sober spirit, be on the alert. Your adversary, the devil, prowls about like a roaring lion, seeking someone to devour. But resist him, firm in your faith... (I Peter 5:5-9a)

There are a number of truths that can be garnered from the wise, old apostle's exhortation. To begin with, these words were aimed at fellow Christians. Yes, God resists pride *even in His own children!* The punishment David faced when he numbered the people is a good example of this. (II Samuel 24:13) Any prideful attitude, motive, or mindset pits us against God. In other words, the more pride one has inside him, the more he will experience resistance by God.

Let's face it: Our Creator insists upon being the master of His people. When a person accepts Christ, he accepts Him not only as Savior but also as Lord.** When that new believer truly surrenders his life and yields to the will of the

---

* His opposition to the pride within a Christian is much different than toward the unsaved. Those who don't know God have nothing to stand between themselves and judgment.

** The term "Lord" is used 7,750 times in Scripture, while the term "Savior" is used only 37 times. This shows the overwhelming weight the Word of God puts upon the Lordship of Christ.

Almighty, his burdens become light and he is full of joy and peace. However, his way becomes hard when he insists upon controlling his own destiny. (Proverbs 13:15) When a man insists upon controlling his own life he finds himself at odds with the entire kingdom of heaven. As one put it: "Think of having the whole of God, his purposes, his laws, his providences, yea, and his love, turned to fight against us." [6] The fact that we are told that He withstands the proud shows how grievous a sin pride is.

Peter also mentions the Lord's care for His people. It is important to remember that He wants to purge everything out of us that would harm us or impede His relationship with us. For instance, many believers do not understand that their prayers go unanswered because they approach the Throne of God with a cocky, presumptuous, and demanding attitude. In their insane pride, they attempt to order the Almighty around as if He is their errand boy! God turns away from such a haughty advance.

One minister explains God's opposition to His own people when they are high-minded: "It is out of loving care for us; it is because pride means rebellion, and rebellion is the very essence of sin; and sin means misery, ruin, death." [7]

It is also interesting to note how Peter's train of thought took him from the subject of pride directly to that of spiritual warfare. There have been innumerable instances in which Satan destroyed believers through their own pride; many are found in Scripture to warn us. One such example is David's transgression. We are told, "Then Satan stood up against Israel and moved David to number Israel." (I Chronicles 21:1) The devil is masterful at coaxing a person to do his bidding by simply appealing to

> "Then Satan stood up against Israel and moved David to number Israel."

27

his pride. This is why the apostle Peter warned his people to vigilantly guard against his attacks. He is a vicious beast who goes to and fro stalking the earth looking for souls to prey upon.

There is no question but that pride is a hideous cancer of the soul that only brings about misery and destruction. Every Christian should feel compelled to rid himself of its evil taint. Let's consider these stirring words from the Pulpit Commentary:

> What have any of us to be proud of? Has the sinner any reason to be proud? He is walking on the broad way that leadeth to destruction. Not a journey, not a prospect, to be proud of, certainly! Has the saint any reason to be proud? Surely not. It is by the grace of God he is what he is. "Not of works, lest any man should boast."... Away, then, with pride! Away with pride of riches! Away with pride of rank! Away with pride of learning! Away with pride of beauty in the face that is made of clay! Away with pride from every Christian heart! Away with pride from the house of God! Away with pride from all departments of Christian work! Away with pride towards our fellow-men! Let us follow in the footsteps of him who was meek and lowly in heart. [8]

∾ৎড়

*Lord, I want this passion in my heart about pride.
Give me a burning desire to come down out of the
lofty heights of pride. I want the lowly demeanor of
Jesus to reign within me. Make it so, dear Lord.
Amen.*

"Pride leads to every other vice: it is the complete anti-God state of mind... each person's pride is in competition with everyone else's pride." [1]
C.S. Lewis

"Think of the power that turned an innocent pink-cheeked boy into a Nero or a Himmler." [2]
A.W. Tozer

t w o

THE FORMATION AND DEVELOPMENT OF PRIDE

THE AMERICAN CULTURE IS PREGNANT with the pride of life. Female beauty is glorified from coast to coast. Physical prowess in sports is given unprecedented acknowledgement. Human ingenuity in science and technology is exalted. Corporate greed is vaunted as shrewd investing. Politicians are praised—not for their integrity—but for pragmatism. Unmistakably, we are under the Darwinian curse of the survival of the fittest.

A few days after the terrorist attack on the World Trade Center, Florida governor Jeb Bush, inflated with national pride, expressed the sentiments of most Americans when he said, "They tried to humble us, but we are a proud people and will never be humbled—we are a strong nation!"* National unity was trumped with such statements as, "We are proud to be Americans!"

Almost everything in our culture caters to and incites man's pride: entertainment, advertising, the media, academics, business and the home life. Now more than ever, it's all

---

* Written from memory by a friend. This is not to infer there is anything wrong with expressing patriotism about our nation.

about image and personal achievement. This, in turn, has created an overwhelming pressure to out-do the next man—to be smarter, stronger, more capable, more attractive, and wealthier.

EARLY LESSONS

In such an environment that exalts and glorifies achievement, strength, and beauty, it doesn't take long for children to learn that it feels good to be praised and hurts to be unnoticed or criticized. They are taught to be proud of who they are and of their abilities. This mentality is reinforced at every stage of development and throughout adulthood.

Take school for instance. As a means of motivation, the first thing teachers appeal to in a child is his pride by sending the message that if he wants to be rewarded by the system, he must *strive* to be the best. He must *out-do* others. He must show a *competitive* spirit. From a biblical perspective, each of these terms is a devilish manifestation of pride.

Early on in life, ambition and vainglory are instilled in children and are considered acceptable motives for doing their best.* Teachers attempt to awaken and stir up the pride that is already inherent in every child. Rather than teaching them godly principles that promote the importance of others, kids are taught that their value comes from *excelling* others. Competition becomes the means to induce young people to do the best they can do. They are encouraged to put themselves in the position of receiving man's applause no matter what the cost. They are told to be content with nothing less than the

---

* It goes without saying that a parent or teacher *ought to* do their utmost to inspire children to do their best. Kids *should be* encouraged to put value in the quality of their work. They are *supposed to* urge young people to become accomplished in a field of interest. However, the current practice of using pride as a tool of motivation is not only unnecessary but is dangerous.

highest distinction. Our country is a country of winners. Losers are second-rate citizens.* Therefore, a person's value is often determined by achievement rather than by moral character.

If a young man shows an interest in some profession, he is taught to emulate successful people in his field: study their lives, imitate their practices, and follow in their footsteps. And the rewards of success—pleasure, possessions, and power—are always in the forefront of his mind. It should come as no surprise that the world would promote these objects as life's rewards. John said, "For all that is in the world, the lust of the flesh and the lust of the eyes and the boastful pride of life, is not from the Father, but is from the world." (I John 2:16) This worldly thinking urges him forward and compels him to work harder. Above all else, this determination to be the top in his field must be accompanied by a positive mental attitude. What glorious things await those who refuse to settle for second best!

Unbelievably, this same mentality is even thrust upon those training for the ministry. Godly characteristics such as love, humility, and kindness tend to be impatiently brushed aside in favor of the outward signs of success. It is usually the most talented preachers that are put on a pedestal. Therefore, our young people aspire to imitate those with the biggest churches, the most popular radio shows, the best selling books, and the most prestigious positions. Bible school students quickly learn that the evangelical system in America richly rewards its darlings. This worldly mindset permeates much of the

> This worldly mindset permeates much of the Church in the United States.

---

* Some in the field of academics attempt to correct this through humanistic methods, i.e. refusing to fail a child who has not met the minimal scholastic requirements.

Church in the United States.

After years of such thorough indoctrination, the majority of young people are governed by greed, envy and self-glory. William Law, writing in the 16th century, asks some troubling questions:

> You teach a child to scorn to be outdone, to thirst for distinction and applause; and is it any wonder that he continues to act all his life in the same manner? Now if a youth is ever to be so far a Christian, as to govern his heart by the doctrines of humility, I would fain know at what time he is to begin it: or, if he is ever to begin it at all, why we train him up in tempers quite contrary to it? How dry and poor must the doctrine of humility sound to a youth, that has been spurred up to all his industry by ambition, envy, emulation, and a desire of glory and distinction! And if he is not to act by these principles when he is a man, why do we call him to act by them in his youth?...
>
> Let those people who think that children would be spoiled, if they were not thus educated, consider this:—Could they think, that, if any children had been educated by our Blessed Lord, or His Holy Apostles, their minds would have been sunk into dullness and idleness? Or could they think, that such children would not have been trained up in the profoundest principles of a strict and true humility? Can they say that our Blessed Lord, who was the meekest and humblest Man that ever was on earth, was hindered by His humility from being the greatest example of worthy and glorious actions, that ever were done by man? Can they say that His Apostles, who lived in the humble spirit of their Master, did therefore cease

to be laborious and active instruments of doing good to all the world? A few such reflections as these are sufficient to expose all the poor pretenses for an education in pride and ambition. [3]

THE JOE BLOWS

In our society, if you want to be respected and admired, you must be the best. The problem is that not everybody can be the best. For every person who is recognized for some achievement, there are usually hundreds whose efforts go unnoticed.

Just like parents reward good behavior and punish bad behavior, pride too is motivated by positive and negative factors. There is an unspoken threat that accompanies the promise of reward for the achiever: if he doesn't succeed, he won't be rewarded. He won't receive the accolades, nor will he reap the benefits of success. He won't be admired by others. He won't be *lifted up* as a shining example for others to imitate.

Most children learn to accept the fact that they were not destined to receive the applause of man. They may secretly envy those who are distinguished, but otherwise, they are content to grab whatever leftovers are available to be had.

It wouldn't be so bad if this were all the Joe Blow types had to deal with, but unfortunately, the problem goes much deeper than this. Humans are born with a deeply felt need to be loved and respected. This desire runs so deep that the lack of noticeable appreciation by others—especially immediate family members—can actually be emotionally damaging to a young child. A child's dependence upon the approval of others or his need for affirmation often creates an overwhelming sense of insecurity. Rather than being self-confident, he tends to be very uneasy around others and is

> He learns early in life to fear emotional pain and avoids it at all cost.

dominated by the fear of man.

Not only does a lack of positive affirmation affect a child, but outright insults or even ridicule from others can intensify feelings of insecurity. He learns early in life to fear emotional pain and avoids it at all cost.

The natural way to deal with the fear of being the object of ridicule is to become someone whom everyone looks up to. Such prominence grants him a certain degree of freedom from the abuse others suffer. Moreover, his "strengthened" position in the hierarchy of his peer group, allows him more liberty to then become the abuser of others.

The young person who knows that he cannot compete at that level must handle these issues differently. When a child doesn't feel as though he's getting the love and acceptance he needs, a sense of inferiority begins to develop within him. This so-called "inferiority complex" is reinforced each time he experiences rejection or is emotionally hurt in some way. The more inferior the child is made to feel by the rejection of others, the more he will attempt to compensate for that lack of security by exalting himself above others and protecting himself from their put-downs.* The child will often seek something—anything—to distinguish himself from others.

Consequently as a child develops, several things begin to happen. Certain forms of pride begin to surface within him in conjunction with his individuality: his strengths, abilities, looks, etc. If he is a sensitive person by nature, he will display self-protective pride to ward off any pain or rejection by others. If he is naturally cocky, on the other hand, he will tend to

---

* Proponents of the "Self Esteem Movement" rightly see the truth of this, but their solution of promoting self only exacerbates the problem.

be conceited and arrogant. The level of his insecurity—his thwarted desire to be highly thought of—usually determines the strength of his pride. Like sin of any kind, pride creates a downward spiral of soul degradation. The more one gives over to pride, the more that pride demands. In other words, it strengthens itself.

The child—who is only doing what comes naturally—gradually develops defense mechanisms to cope with being hurt in life. Unfortunately, these defense mechanisms are the embryos of pride that begin in childhood, are developed in the teen years, and are perfected in adulthood.

In the meantime, the youngster is completely unaware that he is a prime target of demonic spirits. These devils are very familiar with his family tree and all the different personality traits, secret sins, areas of selfishness, and so on. In fact, these agents of darkness have been nurturing sin and pride in members of his family long before he was even born. As the child grows and suffers the inevitable pains of childhood, undoubtedly demons are present to show him how to respond to this pain. *Pride is the devil's solution to emotional pain.* In a fallen, sin-cursed world in which the pride of man is exalted, this ungodly attitude is carefully cultivated as the young person grows into adulthood.

A Lifelong Pattern

Life is a long journey, made up of millions of daily decisions. A person's path can be altered at any time, but the longer he goes in one particular direction, the more inclined he will be to continue in it. Just like an addiction to drugs or sexual activity, the passion of pride can so dominate a per-

> Pride is the devil's solution to emotional pain.

son that it dictates the course of his life. This, in turn, places him in a rut which becomes increasingly more difficult to break out of.

Those deemed insane by society typically have a long history of making decisions that were strongly influenced by pride. If their lives could somehow be examined from the beginning, one would most likely find crucial points along the way where they made choices that further solidified their insanity. The movie *A Christmas Carol* masterfully showed—through the angel of Christmas past—how a young Ebenezer Scrooge made one greed-driven decision after another early in life until he eventually became a bitter, tight-fisted miser.

Every person alive today—whether young or old—is on some course in life and is a product of a lifetime of daily decision-making. People are in a constant state of transition: always changing by small degrees in some particular direction. Consequently, their pride is either mushrooming or diminishing. A.W. Tozer put it this way:

Men and women are being molded by their affinities, shaped by their affections and powerfully transformed by the artistry of their loves. In the unregenerate world of Adam this produces day-by-day tragedies of cosmic proportions. Think of the power that turned an innocent pink-cheeked boy into a Nero or a Himmler. And was Jezebel always the "cursed woman" whose head and hands the very dogs, with poetic justice, refused to eat? No; once she dreamed her pure girlish dreams and blushed at the thoughts of womanly love; but soon she became interested in evil things, admired them and went on at last to love them. There the law of moral affinity took over and Jezebel, like clay in the hand of the potter, was turned to the deformed and hateful thing that the chamberlains threw down from the window. [4]

࿊

*Lord, I now understand more fully why pride has
developed within me. Help me to escape the world's
system of rewarding pride. I don't want the devil's
ugly solution to emotional pain. I want to suffer
like a good soldier of Christ, if need be. I want to
be conformed into His image and transformed from
the devil's. Make it so, Lord.
Amen.*

"There is one vice of which no man in the world is free; which every one in the world loathes when he sees it in someone else; and of which hardly any people, except Christians, ever imagine that they are guilty themselves... The vice I am talking of is Pride or Self-Conceit." [1]

C.S. Lewis

"Pride is a vice which cleaveth so fast unto the hearts of men, that if we were to strip ourselves of all faults, one by one, we should undoubtedly find it the very last and hardest to put off." [2]

Bishop Hooker

three

THE DIFFERENT FORMS OF PRIDE

WHEN ADAM REBELLED IN THE GARDEN, his heart was instantly corrupted. And like an aggressive form of cancer, an elaborate network of pride formed within his heart and spread to his offspring. Now thousands of years later, through countless generations, it contains a highly developed "radar system" which keeps a constant surveillance on everything that comes across its path. Consequently, this built-in mechanism captures every opportunity to vaunt, promote, and protect its host. Thus, pride successfully maintains its fortified position within the human heart.

In essence, pride is like a vicious watchdog, ever protecting its master: the almighty self. The more a person is full of self, the more high-minded he will be. The believer who has not allowed the Lord to deal severely with his "self life" will see all that comes his way through the lens of pride. All aspects of his life—work, amusements, relationships, and yes, spiritual life—will be heavily tainted by pride. His thoughts, words, and actions become polluted by it. Thus, everything must take a subservient position to its tyrannical demands. The unconquered Christian may claim that Jesus Christ is the Lord of his life, but the truth is that pride alone enjoys that position. It rules his heart, gets whatever it demands, and allows only those things that serve its interests. Submission to God is kept at bay outside the boundaries erected by self-love. The believer will only submit and surrender to the Lord as much as self and pride will permit.

It's true. Not only is pride a common feature of man's heart, but every human being—including the believer—has a unique and vibrant self life. Thus, people exalt and guard themselves in many different ways. For instance, each of the six members of the Johnson family is "high" in a way distinct to him or her as an individual. To better diagnose the pride that is within each of us, I will break it down into basic (often overlapping) categories.*

A HAUGHTY SPIRIT

When one thinks of the word haughty, an image of a wealthy snob quickly comes to mind. However, the Bible uses the term to describe any attitude of "being better than others." One need not be rich to be filled with haughtiness. Seeing oneself as smarter, prettier, stronger or more capable than others are all aspects of this kind of arrogance. The one who elevates himself above his fellows experiences a sense of exhilaration.

Bill Johnson is the perfect example of haughtiness. He considers himself to be superior to practically everyone around him—certainly far better than the typical "working Joes" who live from paycheck to paycheck. Even more pronounced is his contempt for poor people "who oughtta' pick themselves up by the bootstraps and make something of

* Some of the concepts written in this chapter originated in a previous book by the author: *At the Altar of Sexual Idolatry.*

themselves!" No matter how he might try to conceal it, his disdain for others comes across in his face. The Psalmist called it "the haughtiness of his countenance" (Psalm 10:4) or a "haughty look." (Psalm 101:5) Solomon simply labeled this look as "haughty eyes." (Proverbs 6:17)

The arrogant person finds something about himself that he deems commendable and then uses that quality to favorably compare himself to those around him. Because he believes the best about himself, Bill overlooks his less desirable characteristics. For instance, he is very demanding as a boss and uses sarcasm to manipulate others to perform his wishes. The truth is that nobody enjoys working for him. In his great desire to think the best about himself, such negative feedback is conveniently ignored. Instead, he congratulates himself on his strong work ethic. Yes, it is true; he is more ambitious than Jim, the custodian who lives down the street. However, everybody who knows Jim loves to be around him, which Bill fails to notice. Superior-minded people exalt themselves by comparing their strengths with the weaknesses of others.

Bill is so smug in his self-evaluation that he is indifferent to the opinions others have of him. His insane arrogance leaves no room for doubt. He is extremely condescending and could care less about what other people might think of him. He scorns their approval just as much as their disapproval. Because of his colossal self-love, he does not require the endorsement of anyone.

VANITY

In contrast to Bill's exaggerated self-confidence is the conceited person who actually lives for the admiration of others. Full of vanity, such an individual craves the approval

> Vanity lies at the foundation of much of the watered down preaching so prevalent today.

of other people, longs to be recognized, and seeks applause.

Vanity lies at the foundation of much of the watered down preaching so prevalent today. Scripture denounces vain preachers who refuse to condemn sin, worldliness, and carnality. Through Jeremiah the Lord said that "...they have healed the brokenness of My people superficially, Saying, 'Peace, peace,' but there is no peace." (Jeremiah 6:14) Jude spoke of those who flatter people. (Jude 16) Paul said, "For the time will come when they will not endure sound doctrine; but wanting to have their ears tickled, they will accumulate for themselves teachers in accordance to their own desires." (II Timothy 4:3) These false teachers want to be liked more than they care about the well-being of their listeners.

Vanity is not limited to the ministry, though. Anybody who craves the admiration of others is susceptible to it. Indeed, it is one of the greatest pitfalls facing women today. A woman's beauty determines her value in our culture. The pressure to be alluring can be very powerful—especially for those who are "needy" for attention. It is no coincidence that the dressing table used by women to apply make-up is called a vanity.

This is especially tragic in the Body of Christ today as young girls—seeking attention from others—dress immodestly even in church. However, the desire for attention from boys too often leads the young girl down the path of promiscuity. Unfortunately, few seem concerned these days as the Church continues to embrace the world's standards.

Vanity puts one in the prison of living his or her life for the approval of others. To maintain that exhilaration of acceptance requires the person to constantly look, speak, and act as others wish him to. The person's contentment depends solely upon his approval rating: praise brings happiness and perceived fulfillment, while a disapproving frown can be most devastating. Perhaps this attitude compelled God (through Isaiah) to admonish, "And the pride of man will be humbled, and the loftiness of men will be abased, and the LORD alone will be exalted in that day... Stop regarding man, whose breath of life is in his nostrils; for why should he be esteemed?" (Isaiah 2:17, 22)

SELF-PROTECTION

An individual with self-protective pride has a very difficult time being vulnerable to others. He is extremely defensive and easily offended. This person has fortified himself with an elaborate system of walls and defense mechanisms in an attempt to keep himself from being at risk. Because the person with this kind of pride is generally sensitive by nature, often the slightest offense will drive him to "save" himself from further harm. Hence, the walls of his personal fortress thicken and become even more impenetrable to any additional "intruders."

Whereas some categories of pride are offensive in scope—such as haughtiness and self-exaltation—this form of pride is defensive by nature. A person with self-protective pride views others as a threat to put him down, belittle him, or make him look bad. Therefore, he guards himself from attacks at any cost. Some insulate themselves from the pain other people may cause by remaining aloof. They are cautious about displaying their true inner feelings and are quite insecure and fearful whenever others come too close. Others use sarcasm to keep people at bay.

Little Suzy, who is only twelve years old, is already allowing this kind of pride to become entrenched inside her. There is nothing wrong with her being cautious, sensitive and introverted. Those characteristics are simply part of her make-up as a person. The problem arises when she—unlike Jesus—gives more importance to her feelings than to the other people in her life. It is easy to sympathize with someone like Suzy until one is on the receiving end of the ugliness that spews out of her when she feels threatened. *PASSIVE RESISTANCE*

The most frightening prospect for the person with self-*REBELLION* protective pride (and for the vain person as well) is to be *SELF* disgraced publicly. The thought of being humiliated in front *DESTRUCTIVE CHOICES* of others is almost more than he can bear. However, Jesus, in addressing the subject of being concerned about what people think, said, "My friends, do not be afraid of those who kill the body, and after that have no more that they can do. But I will warn you whom to fear: fear the One who after He has killed has authority to cast into hell; yes, I tell you, fear Him!" (Luke 12:4-5)

UNAPPROACHABLE PRIDE

A person who is unapproachable does not like to be corrected in any way. He becomes noticeably tense whenever he is admonished about areas in his life in need of change. A proud and foolish person will not receive reproof. Solomon rightly said, "He who corrects a scoffer gets dishonor for himself, and he who reproves a wicked man gets insults for himself. Do not reprove a scoffer, lest he hate you, reprove a wise man, and he will love you." (Proverbs 9:7-8)

> A proud and foolish person will not receive reproof.

It is unfortunate that some people are too proud to be reproved because God tends to be very confrontive in His dealings with those He loves. The writer of Hebrews revealed how God deals with His people: "My son, do not regard lightly the discipline of the Lord, nor faint when you are reproved by Him; for those whom the Lord loves He disciplines, and He scourges every son whom He receives." (Hebrews 12:5-6)

Confrontation of sin by a godly person is one of the most effective methods the Lord uses to bring needed improvement in the Christian's life. Unfortunately, people don't tend to get serious about repenting of sin, selfishness, worldliness, or ungodly attitudes until God sends a Nathan to look them in the eye and tells them the truth about themselves. The Christian who is too high to receive reproof takes himself out of the enviable position of getting God's best for his life; thus, he matures very little. It is as Solomon said, "A rebuke goes deeper into one who has understanding than a hundred blows into a fool." (Proverbs 17:10)

KNOW-IT-ALL PRIDE

The person who becomes high about how much he knows is usually very talented, gifted, and knowledgeable. He tends to think that he can do anything, and in many ways, he often can! He has a great deal of distrust in the abilities of others because of his super-inflated view of himself—his incorrigible ego. Nobody is quite as capable or knowledgeable as he is. This is one of the reasons he does not like to submit to the leadership of others; he thinks he could do a better job if he were in charge. This arrogant attitude makes him rebellious to those above him.

This person's high spirit causes him to consider his own opinions as far superior to the ideas of others. The truth is that he loves to think highly of himself. He tends to think that other people have little to teach him, contemptuously discrediting their abilities and ideas.

This high-minded attitude is censured in Scripture. Solomon said, "Do you see a man wise in his own eyes? There is more hope for a fool than for him." (Proverbs 26:12) Isaiah warned, "Woe to those who are wise in their own eyes, and clever in their own sight!" (Isaiah 5:21) Paul later added, "Let no man deceive himself. If any man among you thinks that he is wise in this age, let him become foolish that he may become wise. For the wisdom of this world is foolishness before God..." (I Corinthians 3:18-19)

REBELLION

No study on pride would be complete without addressing the subject of rebellion. This is especially important in our country because Americans tend to be very independent and rebels to the core! In some ways we have adopted a devilish mindset of questioning authority—God's authority really. People don't tend to submit to leaders anymore than is absolutely necessary. Some simply hate being told what to do.

However, submission is an important part of the Christian life. Believers are admonished to subject themselves to the laws of the land. (I Peter 2:13-14; Romans 13:1-5) Wives are told to submit to their husbands. (I Peter 3:1-5) Workers are encouraged to be in submission to their bosses. (I Peter 2:18) Most of all, believers are encouraged to be in subjection to their spiritual authority. "Obey your leaders and submit to them;" Hebrews 13:17 says, "for they keep watch over your souls, as those who will give an account." Peter said, "You younger men, likewise, be subject to your elders; and all of you, clothe yourselves with humility toward one another..." (I Peter 5:4a)

It goes without saying that a lack of submission to God is another facet of this form of high-mindedness. As it is such an important issue, spiritual rebellion will be addressed later on.

SPIRITUAL PRIDE

Lastly, anyone with a "holier-than-thou" mentality is in the opposite mindset of those Jesus described as being "poor in spirit." The one with spiritual pride imagines himself to be a spiritual giant. God detests self-righteousness and spiritual pride. Jesus was angry with the Pharisees because of their false piety—their outward façade of holiness. They were no less sinful than others around them, but they acted as if they were premier role models of sanctity. However, Jesus had the following to say about them: "Woe to you, scribes and Pharisees, hypocrites! For you are like whitewashed tombs which on the outside appear beautiful, but inside they are full of dead men's bones and all uncleanness. Even so you too outwardly appear righteous to men, but inwardly you are full of hypocrisy and lawlessness." (Matthew 23:27-28)

Many in the Church today act no differently. Some sit smugly in the pews judging everyone around them to see if they measure up to "their standards." Others are the "super-spiritual types" who are always hearing a "word" from God, though their Christian walk is often characterized by instability, compromise, or even outright disobedience. Hence, they are spiritually arrogant, considering themselves to be at a level of maturity at which they have not yet arrived.

A different way people assume too much with God is when they imagine they can continue in unrepentant sin without consequences. They presume upon God's grace. Jude said this about these people: "For certain persons have crept in unnoticed, those who were long beforehand marked out for this condemnation, ungodly persons who turn the grace of our God into licentiousness and deny our only Master and Lord, Jesus Christ." (Jude 1:4) It is one more form of spiritual pride and is extremely dangerous.

This brief examination of pride offers a glimpse at some of the ways it manifests itself within the fallen human nature. Can you see how each of these types of pride limits the Lord from being able to draw near to that person? For instance, is it possible for the haughty-minded man, who exalts himself over those around him, to then be intimate with God? Will the Lord hear the prayers of the self-willed rebel? Will He undertake the cause of the person who protects himself—even if it means being ugly to others—rather than entrusting himself into the hands of the Lord? (I Peter 2:23) No! "God resists the proud," and the greater the degree of pride within a person, the more he will be withstood.

The wonderful thing about the kingdom of God is that sinners can always repent! As you see pride at work in your life, commit yourself to doing all that you can to refrain from following its dictates about how you relate to the Lord and others. God will help you overcome that area of pride—at least to a large degree. It may not automatically disappear simply because you have discovered it is there, but at least seeing it for what it really is will help you fight against it and repent of it whenever it rears its ugly head.

The wonderful thing about the kingdom of God is that sinners can always repent!

༄

Lord, please make real to me every form of pride at work in my heart. Expose each of them for what they are! Help me to become more aware of how pride affects my dealings with You and others.
Set me free!
Amen.

"Pride intensifies all our other sins because we cannot repent of any of them without first giving up our pride." [1]

Life Application Bible

"There is no bottom to pride, there is no height to haughtiness, there is no measure to swelling vanity, there is no temperateness to contempt, there is not 'the bit or rein' that can be reckoned safe to hold in the uncertain, nettled temper of scorn and disdain." [2]

W. Dinwiddle

four

PICTURES OF PRIDE

UNDENIABLY, PRIDE HAS BEEN ONE OF man's greatest downfalls throughout history. While there are many straightforward verses in Scripture on this topic, there is much we can learn from biblical personalities who got caught in the snare of pride and faltered because of it. The Lord's transparency about the spiritual collapse of His choicest vessels is a shining testimony to His own humility and lowliness. For our benefit, He clearly shows us how His Spirit is always in opposition to man's pride. Let's take a look at the lives of three biblical characters and their showdown with the Lowly One.

MIRIAM: FAMILIARITY BREEDS CONTEMPT

Moses' older sister Miriam was certainly one of the most prominent women in the history of Israel. Her courage and quick thinking were already in operation when, as a small girl, she offered to find a nursemaid for the Pharaoh's daughter who had just discovered the baby Moses in the reeds by the riverbank. Eventually she would become a staunch supporter of her younger brother as he faced many trials with the Israelites in the wilderness. She bravely stood by his side and never imagined that she would ever be used by the devil to oppose the man sent by God to lead them to the Promise Land.

In Numbers 11 Moses—obeying the instructions of the Lord—had just appointed 70 elders to rule and judge the people. This was the delegation of authority that Jethro, his father-in-law, had previously advised him to do. Moses, worn out from bearing the weight of the people, was relieved to have others share the responsibility. However, Miriam, who apparently bristled at the thought of losing some of the power she had enjoyed as his confidant, turned on him.

We are told that she and Aaron "spoke against Moses." (Numbers 12:1) It is evident that Miriam was the instigator by the fact that she was mentioned first and was the only one God punished. "Has the LORD indeed spoken only through Moses?" she demanded to know. "Has He not spoken through us as well?" Such sharp questioning reveals that Miriam's close proximity to her younger brother had blinded her to the reality that his walk with God was much deeper than hers. The Lord spoke with him "face to face." (Exodus 15:8) Although she was indeed a prophetess and had stood her ground on the side of the Lord up to this point as others openly rebelled against Him, Miriam made the terrible error of focusing on the humanness of her brother. (Exodus 15:20) Her proud, faultfinding spirit placed her in opposition to God's authority.

Jesus told His disciples "A man's enemies will be the members of his household." (Matthew 10:36) So it is not surprising that this is a common problem amongst the associates of godly men. Because what goes on in one's inner life with the Lord is largely unseen in the daily life, it is easy for assistants to focus on the leader's nature. The shroud of mystery that surrounds Christian leaders is missing for those closest to them. "A prophet is not without honor except in his home town, and in his own household," Jesus told His followers. (Matthew 13:57)

> Having such an enviable position of honor amongst her people affected her spiritually.

There seems to have been two reasons Miriam rose up against her brother. The first was that—as Moses' sibling—she had been exalted in front of over a million people. Having such an enviable position of honor amongst her people affected her spiritually. "Power corrupts and absolute power corrupts absolutely," is an old adage that contains much truth. It is for this very reason that Paul admonished Timothy not to put people in leadership positions too quickly: "...and not a new convert, lest he become conceited and fall into the condemnation incurred by the devil." (I Timothy 3:6)

The second contributing factor can be found in her words: "Has (God) not spoken through us as well?" As a prophetess, Miriam had probably spoken the Word of the Lord on numerous occasions. Perhaps this led her to believe that she was on the same level as her younger brother. John Calvin commented: "They are proud of the prophetic gift, which ought rather to have fostered modesty in them. But such is the depravity of human nature, that they not only abuse the gifts of God towards the brother whom they despise, but by an ungodly and sacrilegious glorification extol the gifts themselves in such a manner as to hide the Author of the gifts." [3]

It is interesting that the following statement is made about Moses: "Now the man Moses was very meek, above all the men who were upon the face of the earth." (Numbers 12:3 KJV) It was meekness that hindered him from defending himself and allowed the Almighty to fight his battles for him. Miriam should have known better, having been an eyewitness of God's fury against those who had scorned her brother's leadership. We are told that the Lord "heard" her words. (Numbers 12:2) His judgment was swift:

> And suddenly the LORD said to Moses and Aaron and to Miriam, "You three come out to the tent of meeting." Then the LORD came down in a pillar of cloud and stood at the doorway of the tent, and He called Aaron and Miriam. When they had both come forward, He said, "Hear now My words: If there is a prophet among you, I, the LORD, shall make Myself known to him in a vision. I shall speak with him in a dream. Not so, with My servant Moses, He is faithful in all My household; with him I speak mouth to mouth, even openly, and not in dark sayings, and he beholds the form of the LORD. Why then were you not afraid to speak against My servant, against Moses?" So the anger of the LORD burned against them and He departed. But when the cloud had withdrawn from over the tent, behold, Miriam was leprous, as white as snow... So Miriam was shut up outside the camp for seven days. (Numbers 12:5-15)

The Bible record shows that on other occasions when Moses was attacked, the Lord responded by utterly destroying people! However, in this situation, Aaron received no more than a sound rebuke and Miriam a one-week case of leprosy. This is a perfect example of how the Lord deals differently with the saved and unsaved. His swift death sentence upon those who attempted to overthrow Moses was to protect the nation as a whole. Rebels who refused to repent eventually received untempered judgment. Miriam, on the other hand, was disciplined as a daughter and restored back into the family.

Nevertheless, the Lord pointedly expressed His great esteem for her brother. One commentator stated:

> The prophets were consequently simply organs, through whom Jehovah made known His counsel and will at certain times, and in relation to special circumstances and features in the development of His kingdom. It was not so with Moses. Jehovah had placed him over all His house, had called him to be the founder and organizer of the kingdom established in Israel through his mediatorial service, and had found him faithful in His service...
>
> Hence Moses was not a prophet of Jehovah, like many others, not even merely the first and highest prophet, *primus inter pares*, but stood above all the prophets, as the founder of the theocracy, and mediator of the Old Covenant... The prophets subsequent to Moses simply continued to build upon the foundation which Moses laid. And if Moses stood in this unparalleled relation to the Lord, Miriam and Aaron sinned grievously against him, when speaking as they did. [4]

Undoubtedly the Lord's praise of Moses was enough to get the attention of his siblings, but Miriam needed to learn this lesson in such a way that she would never forget it. The Lord struck her body with a malignant plague of leprosy. Therefore, because she had exalted herself above God's anointed leader, she was judiciously thrust out of the camp for an entire week—with plenty of time to repent.

Evidently, this humiliation had the desired effect, as we

never again read about her rising up in pride. Surely, the statement is true, "Those whom the Lord loves He disciplines, and He scourges every son whom He receives." (Hebrews 12:6)

SAUL: REBELLION IS AS THE SIN OF WITCHCRAFT

A very vivid illustration of the devastating consequences pride can have on one's life and even on God's kingdom is seen in the life of Israel's first monarch. King Saul certainly *began* his reign in the right frame of mind—he was "little in his own sight." When Samuel told him that he wished to install him as king of the land, he responded by saying, "Am I not a Benjamite, of the smallest of the tribes of Israel, and my family the least of all the families of the tribe of Benjamin? Why then do you speak to me in this way?" (I Samuel 9:21) Later, when the old prophet attempted to anoint him king over Israel, he hid himself.

However, Saul's (human) humility quickly began to dissipate when the Lord gave him a few resounding victories over the enemies of Israel. The first hint that he was rising up in pride came when he presumptuously offered sacrifice to the Lord, rather than waiting as Samuel had instructed him. God rebuked and threatened Saul through the prophet but allowed the misguided ruler to retain his office. The Pulpit Commentary shows the importance of the testing process of the Lord:

> God proves his servants, and does not show them the fulness of his favour and confidence till they have been tested. Abraham was tried and found faithful; so was Moses; so was David; so was Daniel. Abraham, indeed, was not without fault, nor Moses either. David once sinned grievously. But all of these were proved true at heart and trustworthy. Saul is the conspicu-

ous instance in the Old Testament of one who, when called to a high post in Jehovah's service, and tested therein again and again, offended the Lord again and again, and was therefore rejected and disowned. The question on which the king was tested was the same as before. Would he obey the voice of the Lord, and rule as his lieutenant, or would he be as the kings of the neighboring nations and tribes, and use the power with which he was invested according to his own will and pleasure? [5]

Several years passed. More military victories were granted. Now the time had come again to test the character of the theocratic despot and give him an opportunity to redeem himself. After solemnly reminding Saul that God had chosen him as king, Samuel told him to destroy the Amalekite people: "Now go and strike Amalek and utterly destroy all that he has, and do not spare him; but put to death both man and woman, child and infant, ox and sheep, camel and donkey." (I Samuel 15:3) Several hundred years earlier, these bitter enemies of Israel were warned of judgment to come but had never repented of their wickedness. The cup of iniquity was full. They had crossed the line. Now the time had come to fulfill the prophetic warning. (Exodus 17:14) It was Saul's responsibility to completely annihilate the nation.

In spite of his own warnings from God, Saul chose to partially obey, not realizing that partial obedience is actually disobedience. Rather than follow through with the divine executive order to destroy every living thing, he spared the king—as a personal trophy to be showed off—and some of the animals to appease his greedy soldiers. Then, to further kindle the Lord's wrath, he hosted a victory celebration and built a monument *to himself!* "Before his elevation to the royal

> With unmitigated gall Saul exaggerated his obedience and minimized his wrongdoing.

dignity Saul had deemed himself altogether unequal to so heavy a task," remarked one commentator. "Now, after great military successes, he is filled with arrogance, and will rule in open defiance of the conditions upon which Jehovah had appointed him to the office." [6]

When Samuel found him, he immediately confronted him about his disobedience. With unmitigated gall Saul exaggerated his obedience and minimized his wrongdoing. Typical of someone in delusion, he was convinced he was motivated by good intentions. In his mind he had answered the call of God. The fact that he had allowed one man and a herd of animals to live was a trivial detail compared to all that he had done right. "Thus carnal deceitful hearts think to excuse themselves from God's commandments with their own equivalents," quipped one minister. [7]

The penetrating gaze of the solemn prophet should have been a sobering wake-up call in the midst of his sanguine fantasies. The dear old saint, who had spent sleepless nights in agonizing intercession for the rebellious king, did not let him off the hook. "When you were small in your own sight, were you not made the head of the tribes of Israel?" he asked. (I Samuel 15:17 AMP) With that piercing question, Samuel cut this deluded king's heart to the quick. Like Miriam, King Saul had become corrupted by power and had gotten "too big for his britches." He too had a misconception about his relationship to the Lord. But the bleating sheep and the trembling King Agag were an indictment against him.

Saul forgot that his position was merely to be God's visible agent to His people. It was Jehovah who had put him in that position. It was Jehovah who gave him favor in the eyes

of the people. It was Jehovah who had give
over the enemies of Israel. A long and p
awaited him had he chosen to simply obey God's commanus.
Unfortunately, Saul did no more than the bare minimum it
took to get by. Moreover, rather than walk in the fear of the
Lord, he was more zealous to build and promote his own
kingdom apart from God. *Big* in his own sight at this point,
King Saul had abandoned his calling as God's delegated authority over the nation of Israel.

It must have been a chilling scene when Samuel spoke
those immortal words that have challenged many a believer
down through the centuries: "Has the Lord as much delight
in burnt offerings and sacrifices as in obeying the voice of
the Lord? Behold, to obey is better than sacrifice, and to
heed than the fat of rams. For rebellion is as the sin of divi-
nation, and insubordination is as iniquity and idolatry. Because you have rejected the word of the Lord, He has also
rejected you from being king." (I Samuel 15:22-23)

Matthew Henry noted, "that humble, sincere, and con-
scientious obedience to the will of God, is more pleasing
and acceptable to him than all *burnt-offerings and sacrifices.* It is
much easier to bring a bullock or lamb to be burnt upon the
altar than to bring *every high thought into obedience* to God and
the will subject to his will." [8]

Thus, we can see that Saul's great sin against Jehovah was
not so much the fact that he hadn't meticulously performed
every detail he had been told to do. No, the real issue was
that in his heart he had exalted himself against God, "rejected the word of the Lord," and had, in fact, "turned back
from following Him." All of this lay bare to the great
Searcher of souls from whose sight no creature can hide.
(Hebrews 4:13)

We can glean several lessons from Saul's life. First, obedience to God is an issue of the heart. Although Saul ostensibly lived in obedience to Jehovah, this test exposed the true condition of his heart. Saul, like many professing believers, only did those outward acts of piety that would seem to validate his spirituality to those around him. Secretly following the desires of his heart, he—like the Pharisees of Jesus' day—sought the praise of men rather than the praise which comes from God. (John 12:43)

Another key point in this story is that being faithful in the little things day in and day out is far more important than doing great exploits for God. In fact, the truth is that the Lord will never truly use a person in a great way until he learns daily submission. Samuel's words are true: obedience is better than sacrifice.

Probably the biggest lesson we learn from Saul's great fall is the importance of walking "humbly with thy God." Saul had been "small in (his) own sight" at one time, but gradually he became very huge in his own mind. When a person is this way, he is quick to take credit for the good that happens in his life because God has become small in his mind. Thus, he elevates himself and refuses to glorify God. (Romans 1:21) On the other hand, the person who is little in his own sight sees God in everything and is quick to give Him glory. Humble people don't consider themselves to be so.

One final lesson we can derive from this biblical narrative is that delayed judgment will harden an unrepentant heart. Although Saul was rejected as king, he continued on in the office for many years after this. He persisted in his pride and became more callous and insane. But God dealt with Saul like He does with any hard-hearted person who refuses to humble himself: He was very longsuffering. However, it is inevitable that anyone who exalts himself will be humbled, although the outward judgment often doesn't occur for a long time. After the Lord rejected Saul Samuel immediately anointed David to be Israel's new king. But the changeover didn't actually occur for many years. Events set in motion in the spiritual realm often take time to unfold in the physical world. After this incident, God abandoned Saul to the devil, who tormented him for the rest of his miserable life. His mounting insanity eventually brought about his demise. All of it could have been avoided had he simply humbled himself and obeyed the Lord. As the proverb says, "A man who hardens his neck after much reproof will suddenly be broken beyond remedy." (Proverbs 29:1)

NAAMAN: TAUGHT BY SERVANTS

About 200 years later in the land of Syria there emerges "a great man" named Naaman who was "highly respected" because he was "a valiant warrior." Naaman was a national hero and was accustomed to being treated with reverence and respect. He held such status through many courageous and cunning exploits on the battlefield. One can only imagine how many times he had returned to cheering crowds in Damascus after winning great victories for his country. Naaman was truly remarkable in every sense of the word. But just when everything seemed to be going his way, he noticed a white blotch on his skin: the early stages of leprosy!

Little did he know that Jehovah, the God of Israel, had orchestrated a series of events that would give him something more wonderful than all the riches and fame the world had bestowed upon him: a knowledge of God. The story actually began some time earlier when a Syrian raiding party had kidnapped a young Jewish girl and brought her back to Syria where she was purchased by Naaman's wife. Feeling sympathetic to the plight of her new master, the young slave girl mentioned that there was a prophet in Israel who could heal him. The great general, desperate for a medical miracle, was forced to receive direction from a slave! This was the first of several steps *down* for this proud warrior.

In a great display of pomp and arrogance, the mighty man showed up with his retinue of soldiers and aides at the humble abode of the prophet Elisha. Naaman was accustomed to inferiors—such as this Jewish prophet—to bow down in his presence in the most reverential fear. To his shock, Elisha didn't even come out of the house to greet him. Instead, he sent his servant out with a simple message: "Go and wash in the Jordan seven times, and your flesh shall be restored to you and you shall be clean." (II Kings 5:10) The Pulpit Commentary describes his reaction:

> The Syrian general had pictured to himself a very different scene. "Behold, I thought, He will surely come out to me, and stand, and call on the Name of the Lord his God, and strike his hand over the place, and recover the leper." Naaman had imagined a striking scene, whereof he was to be the central figure, the prophet descending, with perhaps a wand of office, the attendants drawn up on either side, the passers-by standing to gaze — a solemn invocation of the Deity, a waving to and fro of the wand in the prophet's hand, and a sudden manifest cure, wrought in the open street of the city, before the eyes of men, and at once noised abroad through the capital... Instead of this, he is bidden to go as he came, to ride twenty miles to the stream of the Jordan, generally muddy, or at least discolored, and there to wash himself, with none to look on but his own attendants,

with no *eclat*, no pomp or circumstance, no glory of surroundings. [9]

Because of his grandiose notions of how his healing should be brought about, Naaman became furious at this treatment. "Are not Abanah and Pharpar, the rivers of Damascus, better than all the waters of Israel? Could I not wash in them and be clean?" he reasoned. (II Kings 5:12) This was a crucial moment. If he allowed his rage to affect his response, he might do something rash like attempt to harm Elisha, who could easily call fire down from heaven to destroy his entire company of men. (II Kings 1:9) However, another one of his own servants came to the rescue and reasoned with him: "My father, had the prophet told you to do some great thing, would you not have done it? How much more then, when he says to you, 'Wash, and be clean'?"

None of this made any sense to Naaman's natural reasoning mind, but nonetheless, his great need caused him to humble himself and obey the words of the prophet who had so disrespected him. He made the two-hour trip down into the Jordan Valley and dipped himself into the river seven times. After the seventh dip down into the murky river, just as the man of God had promised, the leprosy was completely gone. Just like the one cleansed leper who returned to thank Jesus, Naaman traveled all the way back to Samaria to express his gratitude to Elisha. This time, there was no inflated ego or haughty disdain he had previously exhibited. He was a changed man who now experienced the blessing of humility.

There are a number of important things that can be learned from Naaman's humbling experience. The most obvious is that when Naaman had everything going his way, he felt no need to seek out a relationship with Jehovah. It is no

> **The absence of problems tends to make people proud and self-sufficient.**

different today—even with believers. The absence of problems tends to make people proud and self-sufficient. So, in His mercy, the Lord allows adversity to come into our lives to keep us in sight of our constant need of His help in life. (Psalm 119:67, 71)

It is also interesting how the high-minded Syrian general had to constantly receive direction from slaves. First, the little slave girl had to tell him where to look for healing power. Elisha commissioned his slave, Gehazi, to deliver the instructions for the healing. Last, when Naaman went into a tirade, his own servant had to bring the needed wisdom about what he should do. The fact of the matter is that true *servants have a much easier time understanding the Lord because the Kingdom of God is founded upon servanthood*. They have a lowly mindset that the rich and powerful cannot apprehend.

One can also see how different God's ways are from those of man. The Lord gave Naaman a simple thing to do: "Wash and be cleansed." In our human pride, we want to do something that will somehow earn us what we want from God. "If I fast for 40 days surely God will set me free," is the way we often think. But to think this way is to entirely miss the point of the trial, which is to bring about humility and a dependency upon the Lord. Immature, self-centered individuals often want to do some great thing that they can always point to as the reason for their answered prayer. Rather than giving God the glory, the seeker lays claim to it. In Naaman's case, had he been required to do some extraordinary deed to receive his healing, he would have returned to Syria just as arrogant as ever and farther away from God.

Finally, Naaman's seven dunkings in the Jordan in front of his entourage is a beautiful picture of how the Lord helps people come down. Each time he went under, he came that much closer to a knowledge of God. After receiving a sevenfold drenching, he was sufficiently humbled to get a sight of the Lowly One. This simply would not have been possible without enduring these repeated humiliations. Such is the case for believers today. When the Lord allows a person to be humbled in some way, it is always His desire that he come into a greater knowledge of Jesus.

Most people would have thought it impossible for a proud and egotistical man like Naaman to come to God. But the Lord knows exactly how to meet each person's need. In Naaman's case, it took the directions of three slaves and several dunks in the Jordan River to bring him down! But this was a man who was making himself appealing to the Lord. A proud man humbling himself is a beautiful thing in the kingdom of God.

∽↺↬

Dear Lord, I see pride at work in all three of these lives. I desire that you would give me seven "dunkings" or even put me out of the camp for a week, but please God, don't let my pride get so out of hand that you cast me off as you did Saul. Amen.

"An arrogant man stirs up strife, but he who trusts in the LORD will prosper." [1]

Solomon

"Pride is a wonderful artist; it magnifies the small; it beautifies the ugly; it honours the ignoble; it makes the truly little, ugly, contemptible man appear large, handsome, dignified in his own eyes. It is said that Accius, the poet, who was a dwarf, would have himself painted as tall and commanding in stature. In truth, it makes the man who is a devil at heart appear to himself a saint." [2]

D. Thomas

f i v e

RELIGIOUS PRIDE

EXCEPT DURING A FEW ISOLATED PERIODS in biblical history, disobedience and rebellion have been the hallmarks of the Jewish people. This first manifested itself in their participation in the gross idolatry of the pagan nations around them after they had settled into the Promised Land. Their exile in Babylon brought this to an end—they once again cried out to Jehovah. But it wasn't long before a true faith in God was replaced by dead ritualism. At one point the Lord confronted them about their insincere worship when He said that "this people draw near with their words and honor Me with their lip service, but they remove their hearts far from Me, and their reverence for Me consists of tradition learned by rote." (Isaiah 29:13) This was a serious indictment against them, for it exposed that—even in those early days—the Jewish people had become faithless, having exchanged an inward reality of God for outward, lifeless religion.

By the time Jesus arrived on the scene several hundred years later, a cold formalism had become entrenched in Judaism. Rather than keeping the Law out of a sincere devotion to the Lord, the Pharisees had become satisfied with maintaining their religious façades. Jesus hit the nail squarely on the head when He said, "But they do all their deeds to be noticed by men; for they broaden their phylacteries, and lengthen the tassels of their garments." (Matthew 23:5) Everything involved in their ceremonial exercises—whether it was wearing phylacteries or reciting long prayers in public—was done for the purpose of making themselves appear to be spiritual to those around them. Their "faith" had become so corrupted by pride and hypocrisy that—in what seems like exasperation—Jesus exclaimed, "How can you believe, when you receive glory from one another, and you do not seek the glory that is from the one and only God?" (John 5:44) In other words, rather than living to please God—the natural outcome of true faith—the Pharisees built a religious system based upon self-glory and human pride. They were so "high," they couldn't see that God Incarnate was standing right in front of them.

There is no question that the Pharisees* and their "Christian" counterparts, the Judaisers, loomed very large in the minds of New Testament writers, being mentioned over a hundred times. Their presence formed the backdrop of First Century religious life. One of the great struggles of the Early Church was to break away from the external religiosity of Judaism. Fully persuaded that true religion is a matter of the heart, the N.T. writers repeatedly exhorted those first believers to fight for the reality of God in their lives rather than settle for a vain religion characterized by legalism and outward acts of devotion.

Nevertheless, as the Church has evolved over the past two millenniums, the gospel of Jesus Christ has spread throughout the world. As the "wheat" of true Christianity

---

* For the sake of simplicity I use this term in the broad sense to describe all the religious hypocrites of Jesus' day.

has grown, alongside it has grown the "tares" of hypocrisy—those who are content with an outward form of Christianity rather than an inward reality. The postmodern Church has developed its own kind of hypocrisy—tailor-made for today's American life. Although our Evangelical churches don't have ministers parading around with phylacteries and long tassels hanging off their clothes, we have created our own brand

> The postmodern Church has developed its own kind of hypocrisy— tailor-made for today's American life.

of Phariseeism. Religious pride is just as active today as it was 2000 years ago.

EMPHASIS ON APPEARANCES

The first and most obvious characteristic of the Pharisees was that they were far more concerned about how they looked to others than how they looked to God. With laser-like precision, Jesus showed them the spirit they were in:

> "Woe to you, scribes and Pharisees, hypocrites! For you clean the outside of the cup and of the dish, but inside they are full of robbery and self-indulgence. You blind Pharisee, first clean the inside of the cup and of the dish, so that the outside of it may become clean also. Woe to you, scribes and Pharisees, hypocrites! For you are like whitewashed tombs which on the outside appear beautiful, but inside they are full of dead men's bones and all uncleanness. Even so you too outwardly appear righteous to men, but inwardly you are full of hypocrisy and lawlessness." (Matthew 23:25-28)

In this piercing denunciation, Jesus exposed the root cause of their hypocrisy: "they loved the approval of men rather than the approval of God." (John 12:43) Jesus borrowed the Greek word *hypocrite*—used in the Greek world to describe actors assuming a stage role—as the most fitting term available to describe the false piety of the Pharisees. The Jewish world was their stage, and these religious actors had become very adept at playing the part of God's "chosen ones." Their Jewish audience looked to them for guidance and assumed they were leading them in the right direction. The problem was that—much like an influential Hollywood actor might have a script rewritten to make him look better in a movie—the Pharisees had subtly and gradually transformed devotion to Jehovah into a religious system that rewarded outwardness and ignored true inward piety. As Jeremiah said, "they have rejected the word of the Lord," and "the lying pen of the scribes has made it into a lie." (Jeremiah 8:8-9) Ezekiel put it in even more vivid terms, saying, "Her priests have done violence to My law." (Ezekiel 22:26) The transformation occurred so gradually that hardly anybody noticed.

To a lesser degree, this same phenomena has happened in the modern Church in America. Although the Church has had its periods of real revival, this fire has been gradually smothered out by selfishness and worldliness. People naturally take the path of least resistance, but this is the broad way that leads to destruction. (Matthew 7:13) There are many sincere believers who live godly, consecrated lives, but many others have chosen an easier lifestyle and have tried to fit Christianity into their American lifestyle. In other words, like the Pharisees, they too have become professional

> People naturally take the path of least resistance, but this is the broad way that leads to destruction.

religious actors who are spiritually empty inside. Indeed, it is much easier to exaggerate one's godliness than to fight for the real thing.

Jesus warned His disciples about the contamination of false spirituality: "Beware of the leaven of the Pharisees, which is hypocrisy." (Luke 12:1) The best analogy in our day and age to this admonition would be the warnings one might encounter along a highway: "CAUTION! WARNING! STOP! DANGER! WATCH OUT!" For Jesus to use such a strong term as "beware" shows how extremely hazardous He considered hypocrisy to be. The following are some of the reasons it is so dangerous:

- It reinforces a person's self-love;
- It happens automatically when one is high-minded and is hard to detect;
- It substitutes a false spirituality for the real thing;
- It breeds further deception and delusion;
- It hinders a person from seeing his need to change and repent;
- It fosters fear of man rather than fear of God;
- It magnifies the immediate dividends while blinding one to the eternal consequences.

It should be noted that a man's true spiritual condition is not determined by an optimistic self-evaluation. He is not godly simply because he considers himself to be. Nor is he devout because he has fooled others into thinking he is. The reality of his spiritual condition is based upon one thing only: how God sees him. Jesus said, "I am He who searches the minds and hearts; and I will give to each one of you according to your deeds." (Revelations 2:23) The writer of Hebrews said, "And there is no creature hidden from His sight, but all things are open and laid bare to the eyes of Him with whom we have to do." (Hebrews 4:12-13) Everything we do in secret and everything we think (including our secret motives) are all done before the Lord. Those who don't have a reality of the kingdom of God deceive themselves into thinking that their bitterness, lust, greed, self-pity, and envy are insignificant matters. But nevertheless, it all stands out glaringly on the big screen of heaven (as it were) before a holy God. They may convince themselves and others that they truly walk with the Lord, but that doesn't necessarily make it so.

THE EMPHASIS OF SECONDARY POINTS OF LAW

Jesus summarized the true foundation of religion when He quoted the following passage out of the Torah: "'You shall love the Lord your God with all your heart, and with all your soul, and with all your mind.' This is the great and foremost commandment. The second is like it, 'You shall love your neighbor as yourself.' On these two commandments depend the whole Law and the Prophets." (Matthew 22:37-40) Any sincere believer—before or after Calvary—who has conscientiously endeavored to honestly keep these rules of life, has come to know that they are "the great and foremost commandment(s)." He understands that "The one who does not love does not know God, for God is love." (I John 4:8) Therefore, his life is taken up with a deep devotion to the Almighty and is heavily involved with helping needy people, in one way or another.

Although I'm sure the self-deceived Pharisees thought they actually did love God and others, they primarily lived for self. Love for God always translates into the daily life as devotion to others—meeting their needs. (I John 4:20) Since these Jewish religious leaders were closed to sacrificially giving of themselves, they simply avoided the reality of these laws by emphasizing strict adherence to secondary rules. They stressed minor points of the law and de-emphasized the heart-reality of the two greatest commandments. Consequently, over the years they quietly changed the worship of Jehovah into dead ritualism.

One such example was the way they would carefully weigh out their fragments of spice and scrupulously extract a tenth of it to put in the offering. Jesus rebuked them by saying, "Woe to you, scribes and Pharisees, hypocrites! For you tithe mint and dill and cummin, and have neglected the weightier provisions of the law: justice and mercy and faithfulness; but these are the things you should have done without neglecting the others. You blind guides, who strain out a gnat and swallow a camel!" (Matthew 23:23-24)

Modern-day Pharisees don't meticulously weigh out spices, but they still cleverly side-step the fundamentals of Christianity: loving God and others. One such example of this nowadays is the way some over emphasize the importance of doctrine, as if it is the paramount issue of the Christian faith. Much of the disunity and prideful contention alive within 21st Century Christendom is a direct result of those who argue and debate about doctrinal issues with anybody who holds opposing views.

However, a mature, humble believer understands that there is a difference between the *tenets of the faith* and opinions about doctrines of lesser importance. Every born again believer holds certain truths about Christ in common:

- He is a member of the Trinity of God;
- He was God Incarnate;
- He was born of the Virgin Mary;
- He died on Calvary and was resurrected the third day;
- He will return to this earth, (etc.).

These are a few of the important dogmas that form the foundation of the Christian religion. It is proper to "contend earnestly for the faith…" with false teachers who would attempt to overthrow these unshakeable truths. (Jude 1:3) But the problem we have today is that there are those who want to "contend earnestly" with other believers who don't agree with their perspectives about every aspect of Christianity.

Unquestionably, unity is one of the telltale signs of a healthy Church. It means that people are "being of the same mind, maintaining the same love, united in spirit, intent on one purpose." (Philippians 2:2) They are living "With all humility and gentleness, with patience, showing forbearance to one another in love, being diligent to preserve the unity of the Spirit in the bond of peace." (Ephesians 4:2-3)

Jesus prayed that His followers "may be perfected in unity, that the world may know that Thou didst send Me…" (John 17:9) He also said, "By this all men will know that you are My disciples, if you have love for one another." (John 13:35) Given the fact that most Christians frequently have more strife than unity and seem to be more worried about forcing personal opinions upon others than being concerned with the welfare of the needy, is it any wonder that we are derided as self-righteous bigots?

Unnecessary disunity comes about when people place secondary doctrinal issues above the need to love other people and win souls to Jesus Christ. Questions about eternal security, the timing of the rapture, divorce and remarriage, and so on should never separate the saints. It's okay for people to have different viewpoints. However, prideful, immature people cannot tolerate others who dis-

> Prideful, immature people cannot tolerate others who disagree with them on spiritual matters.

agree with them on spiritual matters.

The mature Christian who believes in the tenets of the Christian faith (such as those previously mentioned) has a *godly conviction* that is fortified by *faith*. The person who finds fault with those who take different doctrinal stands has an *intellectual opinion* that is strengthened by *pride*. The humble believer understands that, by and large, he has inherited his viewpoints through his denominational background. For instance, had he grown up in a Baptist church, chances are that he would believe in "eternal security." If he had a Pentecostal upbringing, he would probably embrace an Arminian perspective. Regardless of which opinion he believes, he would not allow it to separate him from other Christians.

Where pride exists people become intolerant of the beliefs of others. By the same token, where humility is given its proper place, unity will prevail. Christian accord and the love of the brethren are more important than one's opinions about secondary doctrines! There's nothing wrong with holding to one's beliefs, but we must be humble enough to admit that our knowledge of the kingdom of God is actually minuscule at best. It is crucial for the sake of unity to focus our attention upon loving God and others. As David points out: "Behold, how good and how pleasant it is for brothers to dwell together in unity!" (Psalm 133:1)

People who only have "a form of godliness" will always seek alternatives to serving God and loving others from a sincere heart. They maintain their spiritual masks and may even scrupulously adhere to certain aspects of Christianity, but they still lack a vibrant relationship with the Lord. Rather than truly submitting themselves to the Lord in all humility, they exert just enough effort to maintain an appearance of godliness. How can the Almighty interact with such hypocrites? He has this to say about them: "this people draw near with their words and honor Me with their lip service, but they remove their hearts far from Me, and their reverence for Me consists of tradition learned by rote." May God have mercy on us and save us from the blinding effects of religious pride!

☙ℰ❧

Dear Lord, please lead me into a living, vibrant relationship with Jesus. Please help me to overcome my natural tendency to present myself as something I am not. Also, give me the humility to resist the temptation to cram my beliefs down the throats of other people. I want to know you in a very real way, Lord. Remove anything from my heart or life that would hinder that from happening.
Thank you.
Amen.

"One step only between haughtiness and hell. Insolent arrogance verges on madness." [1]

J.D. Davies

"Of every proud man God says, 'he and I cannot live in the world together.'" [2]

Jewish Talmud

"Time is on the side of the meek. Time is against the haughty. The judgments of God gather, like black thunder-clouds, against those whose hearts are lifted up. The storm will burst in the ever-nearing future." [3]

R. Tuck

s i x

THE DESTRUCTIVE NATURE OF PRIDE

PRISONS, INSANE ASYLUMS, AND CEMETERIES of the world over provide countless memoirs of souls who discovered firsthand the truth of Solomon's short but poignant statement: "Pride goes before destruction, a haughty spirit before a fall." (Proverbs 16:18) Later on he reinforced this when he said, "Before destruction the heart of man is haughty, but humility goes before honor." (Proverbs 18:12)

I suppose there isn't a spiritual law more constantly confirmed before my eyes than the one put forth in these verses. Everywhere the discerning eye looks, the consequences of high-mindedness stand out glaringly. People by the multitudes have destroyed their own lives and those of others simply because they were unwilling to humble themselves. Pride is to the soul what malignant cancer is to the human body. Not only does it spread throughout one's entire being, but it devastates every aspect of a person's life. Once pride becomes full-blown within the heart unavoidable destructiveness quickly ensues.

Notice that Solomon used the word "before" three times in these two statements. This shows the large part character plays in determining what befalls a person in

> How "high" a person is will determine the consequences he will face.

life. What he *is* governs what he *does*. The person's actions not only establish a pattern of life that reinforces what he is, but they also promote a variety of reactions. Thus, the principle of cause and effect is in operation. *Being* prideful causes the person to *do* certain things, the effects of which bring about terrible consequences. Just like any other sin, pride carries with it its own judgment.

Although the fallout of pride in an unsaved person's life may differ in certain ways from that of a prideful Christian, the same spiritual laws apply to both. Physical, judicial, and spiritual laws all hold one common denominator: they work on the principle of cause and effect. If a man is caught robbing a bank, he will face the full weight of the judicial system. If someone jumps from a tall building, he will be yanked to earth by gravity. If a person exalts himself, he will be humbled. It does not matter if the bank robber, suicide victim, or prideful person professes Christ or not; the cause and effect principle kicks in regardless.

How "high" a person is will determine the consequences he will face. As previously mentioned, pride carries with it its own judgment. Jesus said, "Whoever exalts himself shall be humbled." (Matthew 23:12) Although He didn't tell us how the humbling would come about, it stands to reason that the more pride there is in a person's life, the greater the calamity and disgrace that will come upon him. The following statements made by Solomon supply us with a framework to examine the aftermath of pride:

- When pride comes, then comes dishonor... (Proverbs 11:2)
- A haughty spirit (goes) before a fall... (Proverbs 16:18)
- Pride goes before destruction... (Proverbs 16:18)

THE DISHONOR OF PRIDE

The first spiritual rule of thumb is that pride tends to bring dishonor (Heb. *qalown*) upon a person. Synonyms of this Hebraic term are disgrace, ignominy, reproach, and shame. [4]

Nobody likes the person who imagines himself to be superior to all those around him. There is something repulsive about him. Instead of being treated with respect and honor, the high-minded person provokes ill feelings in other people. What's sad about those who are obsessed with what others think about them is that the more concerned they are about their appearance, the less people tend to respect them. Their prideful attempt to exalt themselves only diminishes their stature in the eyes of others.

The following incident about my wife, Kathy, and myself is a good illustration of this. Several years ago we had dinner with an influential couple I was very concerned about impressing. As we were eating, Kathy told them a funny story about me that embarrassed me. Had I laughed it off, it would have been quickly forgotten, but because I was so concerned about what they thought about me, I got angry. I lashed out at her with a sharp tone of voice. It was an ugly scene, and—because of my pride—the very thing I feared most came upon me—I made myself look bad.

Not only is pride disgusting, it also promotes competitiveness. People who are concerned about self-advancement almost always do so at the expense of others. However, a competition requires an opponent. It isn't enough for a person to gloat over some talent, personal characteristic, or accomplishment. What good is it

> Not only is pride disgusting, it also promotes competitiveness.

if there isn't someone else to defeat or outdo? C.S. Lewis said it like this:

> We say that people are proud of being rich, or clever, or good-looking, but they are not. They are proud of being richer, or cleverer, or better-looking than others. If every one else became equally rich, or clever, or good-looking there would be nothing to be proud about. It is the comparison that makes you proud: the pleasure of being above the rest. [5]

People who view other people as their rivals will inevitably do or say something that will offend them. The words of Solomon attest to this:

- An arrogant man stirs up strife... (Proverbs 28:25)
  Through presumption comes nothing but strife... (Proverbs 13:10)
- Like charcoal to hot embers and wood to fire, so is a contentious man to kindle strife. (Proverbs 26:21)

In each of these three proverbs, conflict arises from a prideful mindset. The outcome is strife (Heb. *riyb*), which literally means "a contest." Since a prideful person is driven to maintain his position above (higher) than those around him, he finds himself in a never-ending competition: everyone is his challenger. It is a battle of wits: he must exalt himself above them and defend himself against their attempts to top him. He views the words others speak with suspicion and tends to be cynical of their motives.

The more a person thinks, speaks, and acts from this kind of a mindset, the more others will dislike him and seek to avoid his company. The person, who lives to outdo others, soon finds himself alone. Mary rightly said that God scatters those who are proud in the thoughts of their heart. (Luke 1:51) Perhaps this happens in large part simply because pride is intolerable in His presence. It brings with it the judgment of dishonor and isolation.

THE INEVITABLE FALL

The second truth presented here is that pride paves the way for a fall. King David is a sad example of this. As a young man, he had utterly humbled himself before God and man. But twenty years of palace life puffed him up quite a bit. Before he saw Bathsheba undressing next door, a devilish idea that he was entitled to anything he wanted had already entered his heart. After all, he was the king! His pride caused him to commit adultery and to deliberately have the woman's husband killed. God thoroughly rebuked him through the prophet Nathan. "Now therefore, the sword shall never depart from your house, because you have despised Me and have taken the wife of Uriah the Hittite to be your wife," the Lord told him. "Behold, I will raise up evil against you from your own household; I will even take your wives before your eyes, and give them to your companion, and he shall lie with your wives in broad daylight. Indeed you did it secretly, but I will do this thing before all Israel, and under the sun." (II Samuel 12:10-12) And that is exactly what happened. The consequences of David's fall from godliness plagued him the rest of his life.

When one thinks of a spiritual leader falling into sin, the first thought is that of moral failure (i.e. sexual sin). But "falls" do not always happen the same way or to the same degree. Some people lose their jobs. Others lose their families. Still

> Gradually, I was slipping away from Him inside.

others are stricken down with illness.

I can give a fresh—and quite literal—illustration of taking a fall out of my own life. Due to a number of reasons, there was a period of several months that I had been overly busy in ministry work. Every weekend I would fly somewhere in the country to speak, only to return on Mondays to run the ministry during the week. Even though I was maintaining my devotional life, the stress and busyness were taking their toll on my walk with God. Gradually, I was slipping away from Him inside. I tried to fight my way back into that place of peace and joy that come from His presence, but it seemed like I was fighting a losing battle. I felt increasingly frantic and agitated inside. All the while I was becoming more high-minded.

Like a man thrashing around in the water, on the verge of drowning, I was in trouble spiritually. I cried out to the Lord for His help, hoping for a divine impartation or a heavenly visitation. His answer came—but not in a way I ever expected!

Kathy and I had decided to do some physical work to alleviate some of my pent-up stress. We began adding a room onto our cabin in eastern Kentucky. One day we installed a window, standing on a makeshift platform next to the house, several feet off the ground. When I stepped on the edge of the platform, it toppled and slid out from under us. And down we both came. My collarbone was crushed and my shoulder was fractured. Kathy received a concussion, four broken ribs, and torn cartilage in her shoulder.

I cannot prove that it was God who threw us to the ground, but I honestly believe that He used it to (literally) bring us down! Kathy and I have expressed our heart-felt gratitude to Him many, many times because that accident got us back on track spiritually. Somehow through the painful ordeal of surgery and weeks of physical therapy and so on, we were calmed down inside, and the reality of His marvelous presence was restored to us. It would be impossible for me to overstate how vital experiences like these are to a person's spiritual life.

Yes, I had risen up inside, but God was faithful to bring me down. "For whom the Lord loves He reproves, even as a father, the son in whom he delights. All discipline for the moment seems not to be joyful, but sorrowful; yet to those who have been trained by it, afterwards it yields the peaceful fruit of righteousness." (Hebrews 12:6, 11) I am grateful because had He not done something to rescue me, I could have eventually had a spiritual fall with devastating consequences.

JUDGMENT AND DESTRUCTION

When the Lord allows calamity to come into the life of one of His people, He does so because He desires to draw them unto Himself and spare them from greater tragedy. Unfortunately, there are many who never seem to learn their lessons. God attempts to speak to them through the Word, through sermons, or even through the admonishment of a faithful minister. He will also allow trials such as the one my wife and I faced. All of this is done (or allowed) with the person's ultimate welfare in mind. However, the price tag can become pretty expensive when a man refuses to heed correction. Solomon said, "A man who hardens his neck after much reproof will suddenly be broken beyond remedy." (Proverbs 29:1)

One example of this is the heartrending story I told in another book about the Major League baseball player who entered the Pure Life Ministries residential program many years ago. Although Eddie Smith (a pseudonym) possessed a number of team records, his career had fallen apart because of his addiction to sex and crack cocaine. The crack had caused him to become so paranoid that he was living in a friend's closet with a loaded gun.

Everything seemed so promising when he began the live-in program. He responded to God's presence at Pure Life in a wonderful way. Spending time in the Word of God every day literally brought sanity to his fearful, tormented mind.

Eddie's greatest problem was not greed, nor worldliness, nor even his obsession with sex. His great, besetting sin was the inordinate amount of pride that had been fostered and nurtured by years of stardom. Even after coming to the place where he was living in a closet with a loaded gun, he remained essentially unbroken. As he began coming back into "sanity," his pride began to rear its ugly head at Pure Life.

At first, it was just over trivial things. He did not like the rules in the live-in program and would simply disregard those which he thought were unnecessary. There is a 10 p.m. curfew in the facility, but if he wanted to eat a snack or talk to one of the other guys, he would do it. When approached about his noncompliant behavior, he would minimize it or shrug it off. As time went on, he grew more arrogant and rebellious. After several months of working with him, his counselor finally attempted a desperate move: he had what is coined a "light session" with him during the Tuesday evening accountability meeting. With Eddie sitting there center stage, each man in the program was asked to share his perspective on the ballplayer's walk with God. Every single man said that he was extremely prideful.

Eddie did not like this very much, but he remained silent. The staff continued their fervent praying for him, hoping that this incident would help turn him around. Unfortunately, his behavior continued to deteriorate after this. Although he was two weeks away from completing the program, I knew I could not graduate a man who was so hard-hearted and unbroken. I reluctantly called him into my office and asked him to leave the facility.

This shocked him. He was not accustomed to people crossing his will like that. He exploded in a rage, saying, "Oh, you're just like the rest, Steve! I hear a lot about mercy around here—but I don't see any!" At this he stormed out and slammed the door so hard that it split the wood on the frame. Eight months later he died of a drug overdose. [6]

God did not kill Eddie Smith; he brought his death upon himself. However, I can attest to the fact that the Lord did everything possible to help him. Godly men had attempted to reason with him. He had brought dishonor upon himself and his family. He had had so many "falls" from grace that he quit counting. This was perhaps his last opportunity to humble himself before the Lord in submission, but he refused to yield one iota. It seems that no calamity was severe enough to get his attention. He was suddenly "broken beyond remedy," destroyed by pride.

While it is never God's desire for people to destroy themselves, humans have a free will that He will not violate. One minister wisely wrote, "There is no field of human thought and action in which pride is not a most dangerous guide. It leads up to and (only too often) over the precipice." [7] Surely it is true, "Pride goes before destruction, a haughty spirit before a fall."

❧

Dear Lord, please, please bring me down! Please root every bit of pride out of my heart and life. I don't want to face destruction and judgment and I trust you to do everything possible to keep me down. Thank you for your chastisement, Lord.
Amen.

PART TWO

THE BLESSINGS
OF
HUMILITY

"The church of God is never so well built up as when it is built up with men of broken hearts. I have prayed to God in secret many a time, of late, that he would be pleased to gather out from among us a people who have a deep experience, who should know the guilt of sin, who should be broken and ground to powder under a sense of their own inability and unworthiness... He who has never been in the dungeon, who has never been in the abyss, who has never felt as if he were cast out from the sight of God, how can he comfort many who are outcasts, and who are bound with the fetters of despair?" [1]

Charles Spurgeon

seven

SAVED THROUGH POVERTY OF SPIRIT

W E HAVE SEEN HOW PRIDE BLINDS AN
individual to his true spiritual condition, how it
distorts his perspective of himself and others,
and how it prevents unbroken fellowship with God. Fortunately, there is a way of escape: through humility. While
there are practical things a person can and should do to
limit prideful behavior and to act more humbly, ultimately,
pride dies as his self-life (i.e. flesh, fallen nature) is dis-
mantled. It is only when a person comes to an end of
himself that his pride is most effectively dealt with and
Christ becomes most glorified in his life. Before we examine the process that brings a person into this blessed
state, let's first take a look at the prerequisites for entrance
into the kingdom of God.

TRUE SALVATION

Today there are billions of wandering souls on the earth,
weighed down with sin, eternally lost, and destined for hell.
Most are heavily engaged in the affairs of this world, completely unaware and unconcerned about their terrible spiritual plight.

Occasionally, God is enabled—primarily through the prayers of saints—to work toward awakening a dead soul. The Holy Spirit attempts to break through the person's spiritual blindness with the reality of his lost condition. He does this by convicting the person of his sin and arranging circumstances that will enable him to see his need for a Savior. As the burden of sin mounts he gradually realizes that he has been in total rebellion against his Maker. John Bunyan masterfully captured the overwhelming despair a convicted sinner experiences in his book, *Pilgrim's Progress* as "Christian" frantically searches for a way to unload the weight of his sin.

When a person recognizes his spiritual impoverishment he knows that there is nothing he can do to save himself. He is utterly undone over his condition. "Blessed are the poor in spirit, for theirs is the kingdom of heaven," Jesus exclaimed. (Matthew 5:3) He is, as it were, flat on his face with nowhere else to turn for help but to God. His destiny is completely out of his hands. In utter desperation, he must approach the Almighty with nothing but a plea: "Have mercy upon my wretched soul!" This is the only entrance into the kingdom of heaven.

It is at this point that a person has spiritually "hit rock-bottom"—he's no longer high! When a repentant sinner has exhausted every possibility of helping himself, he throws himself into the arms of the Savior. It is there at the foot of the Cross that the person must make a genuine decision for Christ. Songwriters of old beautifully testified of this precious moment:

Long my imprisoned spirit lay,
Fast bound in sin and nature's night;
Thine eye diffused a quickening ray,

I woke, the dungeon flamed with light:
My chains fell off, my heart was free,
I rose, went forth, and followed Thee. [2]

Mercy there was great and grace was free;
Pardon there was multiplied to me;
There my burdened soul found liberty,
At Calvary. [3]

Realizing one's need doesn't automatically guarantee procurement of eternal life. Many come to that place only to turn away, unwilling to acknowledge and repent of their sins and make the required surrender. Apparently this is what happened to the rich young ruler. Unsure of his eternal destiny, he prostrated himself before the Savior of souls and asked what he must do to be saved. However, when Jesus put His finger directly upon the idol which blocked his true surrender—coveting lust—we are told that "his face fell, and he went away grieved, for he was one who owned much property." (Mark 10:17-22) This man was brought face-to-face with his spiritual need, but when it came right down to it, he was unwilling to part with "the things of this world" that held him in bondage.

You see, realizing one's hopeless condition is only the beginning. The bondage to sin, self-determination, and the love of the things of this world must be broken in a person. If the seed of the gospel is planted into the soil of a "good heart" (Luke 8:15)—that is, a responsive heart—then the reality of what he's like overwhelms him, and he grieves in deep, inner anguish over his wretched condition. He moves beyond simply seeing his helplessness to *responding* to the guilt he feels about having rebelled against a holy God. He breaks over his sinful state; in other words, he repents. This person now crosses the defining line into a new life in Christ.

THE APPROACH TO GOD

Tragically, there are many who have "made a decision for Christ" but have never experienced this kind of genuine repentance and surrender. Can it truly be said of them "theirs is the kingdom?" They may have entered the Evangelical Movement, but the prideful self that has spent a lifetime defying the Lordship of Christ still remains unbroken. With the proud self securely on the throne of their heart, they see no need to relinquish control and yield to the Greater One. Thus, self reigns as dictator, approving or denying any requirements the Word of God or the Holy Spirit might make of them. They are unbroken, unrepentant and unsurrendered.

In the story of the Pharisee and the publican found in Luke 18, Jesus exposed this false approach to Christianity while contrasting it with true conversion. Luke writes that He "told this parable to certain ones who trusted in themselves that they were righteous, and viewed others with contempt." Consequently, this story confronts those who have never transferred their trust and dependence from self to God. Jesus begins the parable by describing the Pharisee's approach to his Maker: "Two men went up into the temple to pray, one a Pharisee, and the other a tax-gatherer. The Pharisee stood and was praying thus to himself, 'God, I thank Thee that I am not like other people: swindlers, unjust, adulterers, or even like this tax-gatherer. I fast twice a week; I pay tithes of all that I get.'"

Jesus exposed the self-righteousness

> This person now crosses the defining line into a new life in Christ.

of the religious leaders of His day through this proud, unbroken Pharisee. Like many today, he had a grandiose attitude and was quite self-absorbed. He was quick to point out all of the positive things he had done in the Kingdom of God. Unfortunately, he was completely blind to the fact that his entire spiritual

> He came with the attitude that the Lord was fortunate to have such a follower as he.

experience was rooted and grounded in nothing but self. No wonder he basked in his own self-glory. A sense of need never brought him to his knees.

By today's outward standards, the Pharisee lived a godly life: praying, fasting, tithing, and abstaining from obvious, visible sin. He carefully gave God all the credit for the success he achieved. It is interesting to note that when he took a personal inventory of his life, everything he saw about himself was positive. He would easily fit in with our contemporary evangelical "hype movement," which promotes a false gospel based upon emotions, feelings and maintaining a positive mental attitude.

It is also obvious that this Pharisee had little fear or reverence for God. Self-love had blinded him to the point that the Almighty was quite small in his mind, while he was huge. He did not draw near to the throne of heaven with the humble and submissive attitude of a subject before his king. Rather, he came with the attitude that the Lord was fortunate to have such a follower as he. With such an exalted view of himself, it is easy to see how he could demand that God honor his every request.

The approach of the other man was quite different: "But the tax-gatherer, standing some distance away, was unwilling to lift up his eyes to heaven, but beat his breast, saying, 'God, be merciful to me, the sinner!'" This man did not march into the throne room of God and demand His undivided attention. In fact, he stood off in the distance, unwilling even to look up at the Lord. He was overwhelmed by his own unworthiness as he stood in the presence of the Almighty. His sins were "ever before" him as he bowed in the presence of the Holy One. He was sorrowful over his lack of Christlikeness, and deeply regretted how little he had done for God. Nevertheless, he stood there looking for one thing: mercy.

Nowadays, those from an upbeat church atmosphere might suggest that this man simply needs to be reassured about who he is in Christ. Perhaps they would berate him for his negative attitude and label him as a spiritual loser living a defeated life. "You are a child of the King and should think of yourself in such terms," they would exclaim. "You just need to accept God's love and learn how to forgive yourself. You need to speak with faith!"*

It's interesting how heaven's perspectives can be different from earth's. George Whitefield, the fiery preacher of the Great Reformation and one of the greatest soul winners in the history of the Church, had tremendous spiritual insight concerning salvation. He knew what the real thing looked like. He had this to say about the publican:

> Poor heart! What did he feel at this time! None but returning publicans, like him, can tell. I see him standing afar off, pensive, oppressed, and even overwhelmed with sorrow; sometimes he attempts to look up; but then, thinks he, how shall such a wretch as I dare to lift up my guilty head!

---

* Some of this material has been extrapolated from *Living in Victory*, written by the author.

And to show that his heart was full of holy self-resentment, and that he sorrowed after a godly sort, he smites upon his breast, his treacherous, ungrateful, desperately wicked breast; a breast now ready to burst: and at length, out of the abundance of his heart, I doubt not, with many tears, he at last cries out, God be merciful to me a sinner, a sinner by birth, a sinner in thought, word, and deed; a sinner as to my person, a sinner as to all my performances; a sinner in whom is no health, in whom dwelleth no good thing, a sinner, poor, miserable, blind and naked, from the crown of the head to the sole of the feet, full of wounds, and bruises, and putrefying sores; a self-accused, self-condemned sinner.

"I tell you," says our Lord, "this man," this Publican, this despised, sinful, but broken-hearted man, "went down to his house justified (acquitted, and looked upon as righteous in the sight of God) rather than the other." [4]

THE BLESSEDNESS OF POVERTY

Those who have said the sinner's prayer but have not yet experienced genuine repentance—coming to an end of oneself, godly sorrow over sin, brokenness, and surrender—have a difficult time grasping the blessings this broken and contrite publican received. They have never felt the need to throw themselves upon the mercy of God. Indeed, they have spent a lifetime justifying themselves and avoiding the reality of their true spiritual condition. Perhaps they initially shed a few glaring bad habits and made some alterations to their lifestyles so that they might fit into the evangelical culture, but for the most part they

> How different are those who have become absolutely undone over their sin.

continued to give self full sway in much the same manner as before they made their profession of faith.

How different are those who have become absolutely undone over their sin. I recently received a letter from a man in a homeless shelter who had just read my first book, *At the Altar of Sexual Idolatry*. His story is a picture of what real repentance looks like:

I am not new at the self help games and the Jesus help game and have read lots of books on spiritual warfare, inner healing, and such.

Your book, is without a doubt the clearest, most accurate, most genuine, most in my face and heart book I've ever read! It was like you grew up with me! It was like reading my life story! The more I read, the more I recognized parts of me, my behaviors, attitudes, my sick, sick self that I have never been able to define or had anyone else define either. The more I read the more convicted I became and the more the blinders came off and I was finally face to face with the cause of my sin.

Your book laid it out for me without tiptoeing around and God showed me myself: selfish, arrogant, proud, and habitually addicted, with absolutely no self-control. No lie; I put the book down when I read and realized it was my fault all along and sobbed uncontrollably in the most broken and humble, actual godly sorrow, repentance session I have ever experienced.

This man, like the publican, came to "the end of his rope."

The all-seeing eye of the Holy Spirit flashes the light of His gaze deeply into a man's sin-infested soul and exposes everything there. The Lord, in His mercy, presents him with evidence concerning his true state of being. The painful truth about how ugly he is inside horrifies him. All seems lost. The future is nothing but dark gloom. He feels hopeless and helpless. He knows he is in deep trouble and has nowhere to go. But it is at precisely this point that he *turns to God*. Deep within his heart he renounces and abandons the sin and self-will he has cherished.

Suddenly, everything is different. All the obstacles that have kept him at a distance from God are removed. There is now nothing hindering him from the Savior. He throws himself into the heavenly Father's arms and is instantly enveloped in His glorious presence. Tears of despair become tears of joy! Indeed, all heaven is rejoicing over his penitence. (Luke 15:7)

As the soul-blinding effects of his sin and pride are wiped away, he discovers a heavenly perspective he never had before. He is in the glow of the "first love" where everything seems fresh and new! The grass is greener and the sky bluer than ever before. The Word of God, which had seemed stale and lifeless, is now energized, virtually jumping off the page into his heart. The presence of God is sensed everywhere he turns. His worship comes alive as he sings from a rapturous heart. He sees people differently as well. Instead of seeing them through the eyes of self—that dark perspective that reduces others to rivals who must be outdone—he sees their needs. He feels compassion and love for them.

His view of God undergoes a radical transformation as well. He no longer needs a Bible teacher to explain the eternity-determining verdict pronounced by Jesus: "Truly I say to you, whoever does not receive the kingdom of God like a child shall not enter it at all." (Mark 10:15) That statement is more real than life. He *feels* like a child. He has a new sense of child-like trust for the heavenly Father. He is prepared to submit himself to the Lord like any obedient child would. Just as a little boy looks to his parents for the sustenance of life, he fully expects God to meet his needs.

It is there, at the foot of the Cross, that the first blessings of humility are discovered. Those who waste their lives looking for happiness and fulfillment outside of their relationship with God can never understand the unspeakable joy to be found in Him alone. Only those who repent like the publican know the ineffable bliss of such a life.

Perhaps this would be a good opportunity for you, the reader, to consider whether or not you have "gone down to (your) house justified." Have you come to an end of self-will? Have you allowed Jesus Christ to take His rightful place on the throne of your heart? Have you truly surrendered to Him and made Him the Lord of your life? Answering these questions honestly and making sure your surrender is complete is the best way to receive the truths found in the rest of the book.

⁌⁍

Dear Lord, I acknowledge that I know very little about poverty of spirit, sorrow over sin, and true repentance. Please, please bring me to that place of self-nothingness. I am fed up with self-based religion. I want to be like this publican. Please bring me to an end of myself, no matter what the cost. I will not let go of You until I receive what I need.
Amen.

"Brokenness is the way of blessing, the way of fragrance, the way of fruitfulness... Meekness is the sign of brokenness." [1]

Watchman Nee

"How few of the Lord's people have practically recognized the truth that Christ is either Lord of all or He is not Lord at all! If we can judge God's Word, instead of being judged by it, if we can give God as much or little as we like, then we are lords and He the indebted one, to be grateful for our dole and obliged by our compliance with His wishes. If on the other hand He is Lord, let us treat Him as such." [2]

Hudson Taylor

eight

MEEK BEFORE GOD

MAN IS A REBEL AND THE OFFSPRING OF a race of rebels. Thus, he naturally follows the "course of this world, according to the prince of the power of the air, of the spirit that is now working in the sons of disobedience." (Ephesians 2:2) Lucifer established this worldly pattern long ago after his unsuccessful attempt to forcibly overthrow heaven's government so that he could usurp God's rule and authority. Discontent to simply walk in the presence of his Creator, he lusted for position, power and prestige and became absolutely insane.

How utterly different is the mindset of the meek and lowly Jesus. He enjoyed all heaven's highest privileges. He basked in the adoration of the angelic hosts and lived in perfect, loving harmony with the Father. Yet, He gave all this up in order to meet the need of sinful mankind. Paul said, "Have this attitude in yourselves which was also in Christ Jesus, who, although He existed in the form of God, did not regard equality with God a thing to be grasped (i.e. insisted upon keeping), but emptied Himself (His position and privileges), taking the form of a bond-servant, and being made in the likeness of men. And being found in appearance as a man, He humbled Himself by becoming obedient to the point of death, even death on a cross." (Philippians 2:5-7)

Jesus once said, "I always do the things that are pleasing to Him." (John 8:29) Consequently, He never rose up inside. This kind of heart obedience is our model of true meekness—*the willing submission of one person to the will of another.* It is the opposite of self-will, self-determination, and rebellion. A vivid picture of such meekness is seen at Gethsemane: "Father, if Thou art willing, remove this cup from Me; yet not My will, but Thine be done." (Luke 22:42)

THE SOLDIER MENTALITY

Scripture commands believers to submit to God. (Ephesians 5:24; James 4:7; Hebrews 12:9) The word submit (Gk. *hupotasso*) is a conjunction of two other words: *hupo*, which means "under" and *tasso*, which means "to arrange," thus, "to be arranged under or in subjection to the leadership of another." The best illustration of it is an army assembled in marching formation. Every man is submitted to his superiors.

However, imagine there was one private straggling outside the ranks, walking along at his own pace, sometimes in formation but most of the time just doing his own thing. The general, seeing the self-will and unsubmissiveness in this private's life, could never trust him to follow orders. How would he respond to that soldier if he approached him requesting something? He would probably be so disgusted with his willfulness and audacity that he would simply walk away from him. Wouldn't it be appropriate for the general to *resist* the insubordinate private?

> A good soldier, on the other hand, obeys out of respect and devotion to his leader.

A good soldier, on the other hand, obeys out of respect and devotion to his leader. He places himself under the leadership of his commander—not only outwardly but also *in his heart*. It is more than simply obeying out of fear of the consequences for disobedience. He is committed to his leader's cause. In reality, he has renounced his own will in favor of that of the general. His attitude has earned him the trust of his superiors, and he is thereby granted a position of responsibility.

As Christians, we face a daily battle to remain submitted to the Holy Spirit. The flesh always wants to be in control and fights against one's sincerest efforts to live in the Spirit. Paul made a very profound statement regarding this: "For the mind set on the flesh is death, but the mind set on the Spirit is life and peace, because the mind set on the flesh is hostile toward God; for it does not subject (*hupotasso*) itself to the law of God, for it is not even able to do so; and those who are in the flesh cannot please God." (Romans 8:6-8)

How does the Lord bring an independent person into real submission? The same way the Army transforms a raw recruit into a disciplined fighter: the beginner's self-will must be crushed, and he must learn to align himself with the will of his superior.

THE IMPORTANCE OF BROKENNESS

Until a believer's life is under God's control, he is of little use to His kingdom. The only way he can come into meekness is through the breaking of his will. A good analogy of this is that of a wild stallion. It may be a beautiful and graceful animal, but it has no usefulness in its untamed condition. But, once it has been broken, the powerful horse is controlled and led by the reins and verbal commands of its master.

The Christian whose will has been crushed by his heavenly Father develops a healthy respect for the Master's whip.

> "The Lord is near to the brokenhearted, and saves those who are crushed in spirit."

He does not exhibit the cowering fear an abused child has of a cruel father, but instead, he shows proper reverence for One who commands respect. Because his will has been conquered, he no longer sees his life as one in which he has the right to control. David was such a man. Even as the Lord rebuked him (through Nathan) for the Bathsheba affair, He revealed what a special place David had held in His heart: "It is I who anointed you king over Israel and it is I who delivered you from the hand of Saul. I also gave you your master's house and your master's wives into your care, and I gave you the house of Israel and Judah; and if that had been too little, I would have added to you many more things like these!" (II Samuel 12:7-8) Up until the time he reached the pinnacle of pride and fell into the precipice of sin, David had enjoyed a tremendous degree of God's favor.

One of the things David said to the Lord when he dropped to his knees in deep penitence over his sin was this: "The sacrifices of God are a broken spirit; a broken and a contrite heart, O God, Thou wilt not despise." (Psalm 51:17) On another occasion, he used these same adjectives: "The Lord is near to the brokenhearted, and saves those who are crushed in spirit." (Psalm 34:18) The Hebrew terms translated as broken (*shabar*) and contrite or crushed (*dakah*) are extremely important for the one who wishes to be highly esteemed by God. It is very interesting how *shabar* is used elsewhere in the Old Testament.

- Throughout Egypt hail... beat down everything growing in the fields and stripped every tree. (Exodus 9:25)
- You must demolish (their idols) and break their sacred stones to pieces. (Exodus 23:24)

110

- The LORD has given him over to the lion, which has mauled him and killed him. (I Kings 13:26)

Thus, *the Lord is most drawn to and infatuated with the one whose self-life has been crushed, beaten down, broken to pieces, and mauled.* These terms describe a person whose heart condition is diametrical to that of a person who is strong in himself (remember Uzziah?). Many want that special position with the Lord (even imagine that they have it), but how few are willing to allow the Lord to break them in this way.

The Lord is drawn to the lowly. People who have allowed the hardships of life to break down the hard shell of self have the tenderest hearts in the kingdom of God. No wonder God finds them irresistible! The Lord proclaimed through the prophet Isaiah: "For thus says the high and exalted One who lives forever, whose name is Holy, 'I dwell on a high and holy place, and also with the contrite (*dakah*) and lowly of spirit in order to revive the spirit of the lowly and to revive the heart of the contrite (*dakah*)." (Isaiah 57:15) Watchman Nee, in his excellent book *The Release of the Spirit*, says the following:

> To break our will, God must strike us with a heavy blow until we prostrate ourselves in the dust and say, "Lord, I dare not think, I dare not ask, I dare not decide on my own. In each and every thing I need Thee." In being thus stricken, we learn that our will is not to act independently of God...
>
> All who are broken by God are characterized by meekness. Formerly, we could afford to be inflexible and obstinate, because we were like a house well buttressed by many supporting walls. As God removes these walls one after another, the house is bound to

collapse. When the supporting walls are toppled, the interior strength of self cannot but fail. ³

CONFORMING TO THE WILL OF GOD

As the Holy Spirit begins the process of breaking the believer of self-will, He also starts erecting boundaries in his life. Before the person came to Christ, he was free to do as he pleased. Other than certain expectations placed upon him by his boss or family, he really didn't have to answer to anybody.

Now he finds that he must submit himself to the will of another and soon discovers that new restrictions have been placed upon him. He can enjoy life, but only within the limits prescribed by his new Master. As he matures in the faith, he finds that those encircling boundaries become more restricting. Over the course of time, the believer is increasingly reined in, as the Lord gradually exerts His will in his life.

Many biblical characters experienced this divine hedge of protection. Job complained, "He has walled up my way so that I cannot pass." (Job 19:8) David exclaimed, "Thou hast enclosed me behind and before, and laid Thy hand upon me." (Psalm 139:5) Jeremiah said, "He has walled me in so that I cannot go out. He has blocked my ways with hewn stone." (Lamentations 3:7, 9) In regards to faithless Israel, the Lord stated, "I will hedge up her way with thorns, and I will build a wall against her so that she cannot find her paths." (Hosea 2:6)

Most of the time the Christian is oblivious to these invisible parameters in his life.

These statements reveal the different ways in which the Lord establishes borders around the lives of His followers. Most of the time the Christian is oblivious to these invisible parameters in his life. It is only as he attempts to go beyond those divinely imposed limitations that he becomes aware of them.

Some people become aggravated over such restrictions. Determined to have their own way, they continually fling themselves against the wall, many times banging their heads repeatedly. But God is at work in their lives and is trying to lead them into the peace that comes through obedience. As one minister stated: "The wandering sheep is torn by the hedge, while the quiet, obedient sheep knows nothing of the briars." [4]

At first, the primary purpose for the boundary is to keep the new Christian from doing foolish things that will harm him. Solomon said, "Like a city that is broken into and without walls is a man who has no control over his spirit." (Proverbs 25:28) An undisciplined Christian is an open target for the enemy. Fortunately, God's grace will help keep him on track.

However, there is much more to this process than simply having one's actions restrained. It is the Lord's desire that the believer matures, develops his own convictions, and is actually content and pleased to do God's will. When a person's will is swallowed up in the Lord's, the two wills are assimilated into one. The two beings become one.

In biblical times when two people were married, the woman understood that she was joining her life to her husband's. Today in America, marriage is more of an equal combining of two lives, two careers, and two sets of desires. The role of the wife in biblical times was only a step above that of the family servant. The wife forfeited her dreams and aspirations to attach herself to the husband's. She became his mate and submitted her will to his. There was a union of two wills, but it was almost a complete subjection of one to the other.

We, as the Bride of Christ, are called to abandon our own interests, plans, and goals and subject them to our Lord and Husband. It is His responsibility to provide for us, protect us, and bring fulfillment to our lives. When we marry Him, we align our lives with His plans, submit our wills to His, and live within the confines of this marital contract.

Every Christian is offered the astounding blessing of being united in extreme intimacy with the most lovely, decent Person who has ever lived. Who wouldn't be ecstatic to receive a dinner invitation at the White House? No personal sacrifice would be considered too high for such a privilege! How much greater the honor it is to be utterly intimate with Jesus Christ—to be considered His dear friend and even lover. He desires that every believer would come into that special relationship where He shares His most private thoughts and intimate details.

This is an open invitation. "Come unto me, all ye that labour and are heavy laden, and I will give you rest. Take my yoke upon you, and learn of me; for I am meek and lowly in heart: and ye shall find rest unto your souls. For my yoke is easy, and my burden is light." (Matthew 11:28-30 KJV) Yes, there is a yoke for followers of Christ. We must obey God and put our necks under the control of the Holy Spirit. God must be given the right to crucify the self-will within us and to rein us in. However, the benefits of such a close union with Christ are inexpressible! It involves the liberation from the ponderous, soul-draining weight of pride and self-will. To truly be yoked with Jesus Christ means to soar with Him like an eagle! It is this kind of relationship that Jesus tells us we need to learn about and desire.

Conquered by God

One historical figure who became close to the Lord in this way was Moses. He is the most predominant figure of the Old Testament, having written its first five books and being mentioned nearly 800 times in Scripture. He was the vessel God used to bring the plagues on Egypt that brought about the deliverance of His chosen people from bondage. He was also used to establish the nation of Israel and to form the Jewish religion. However, this chosen vessel needed extensive spiritual preparation for this great undertaking.

Moses was raised in the palaces of Egypt, a civilization that was far ahead of its time in many areas of knowledge such as pathology, astronomy, and engineering. Unfortunately, it seems that this extraordinary wisdom came from knowledge of "the deep things of Satan." This evil empire was undoubtedly controlled by "the world forces of this darkness... the spiritual forces of wickedness in the heavenly places." (Ephesians 6:12)

Unquestionably, it was a foul and exceedingly depraved world in which Moses grew up. As a member of the Pharaoh's household, the young Hebrew received a thorough indoctrination, having been "educated in all the learning of the Egyptians." (Acts 7:22) By the time he was forty, he was steeped in the satanic mindset of Egypt. However, it was at this time, that he had an encounter with God that completely changed the course of his life. *The Amplified Bible* beautifully expresses the consecration Moses made when he received this revelation of Jehovah:

> [Aroused] by faith Moses, when he had grown to maturity and become great, refused to be called the son of Pharaoh's daughter, because he preferred to

share the oppression [suffer the hardships] and bear the shame of the people of God rather than to have the fleeting enjoyment of a sinful life.

He considered the contempt and abuse and shame [borne for] the Christ (the Messiah Who was to come) to be greater wealth than all the treasures of Egypt, for he looked forward and away to the reward (recompense).

[Motivated] by faith he left Egypt behind him, being unawed and undismayed by the wrath of the king; for he never flinched but held staunchly to his purpose and endured steadfastly as one who gazed on Him Who is invisible. (Hebrews 11:24-27)

The Lord was preparing to bring His people into the Promised Land. His laws would govern this new nation. To accomplish this He had to have a man who understood obedience—not simply the outward obeisance to rules—but a deep, heart-felt conviction to obey Jehovah. Moses was chosen from birth to be that man. Unfortunately, he—like the rest of his fellow countrymen—was an inveterate rebel. He became zealous for the Lord, but he was so full of self-righteousness that he murdered an Egyptian man. He would have to undergo a deep change of character before he could teach others about obedience.

Scripture is strangely silent about Moses' sojourn on the backside of the desert. One can only imagine what God put him through to prepare him for the overwhelming challenge that lay before him. For forty years Moses was disciplined, humbled, hemmed in, and broken by God. He had to be purged of his Egyptian mentality and to learn how to obey Him. At any rate, it was a completely transformed man who walked into Pharaoh's palace forty years after he left in disgrace. The Bible tells us that he "was very meek, above all the men that were upon the face of the earth." (Numbers 12:3) To say it another way: *The inner life of Moses was more subdued, controlled, and taken over by the Holy Spirit than anyone else alive.* He had become so purified in the Refiner's fire that he was able to speak with the Lord face to face. (Matthew 5:8)

The 21st century Christian is not likely to have the kind of encounters with the Almighty that Moses had. However, the same spiritual principles are in effect today as then. The more the Holy Spirit conquers a person inside, the closer that person comes to God. The deeper a person's submission, the greater will be his revelation of God. His heart will perceive, his ears will hear, and his eyes will see the spiritual realities of the invisible world in which Jehovah reigns. (Matthew 13:14-16)

Everything involved with Christianity revolves around a person's relationship with Christ, which in turn depends upon his level of subjection to God. As the believer becomes progressively more submitted to the Lord's rule in his life, he will find the reality of God growing within his being. There is no shortcut to such precious intimacy.

❧❧❧

Dear Lord, I offer my body, my soul, my mind, my heart, my will, my desires and my dreams as a sacrifice on your holy altar. Please break open my hard, unyielding self. Bring me into subjection to the Holy Spirit. Thoroughly conquer my inner man. Lord, do not ever let me have my way if it will bring disgrace to Your name, will hurt Your people, or will harm me eternally. I give You permission to do anything necessary to keep me in Your precious will.
Amen.

"It has the appearance of a contradiction in terms but is nevertheless true, that he who walks in humility walks in power." [1]

George Ridout

"The first, second, and third thing in religion is humility; and no one ever becomes a Christian who is not willing to take the lowly condition of a child." [2]

Albert Barnes

"It is very difficult to compete with someone who chooses to be last..." [3]

Gayle Erwin

nine

WALKING IN HUMILITY

W HEN A PERSON UNDERGOES THE
Lord's discipline and experiences the breakdown
of his self-life and the pride that thrives within
it, he will become increasingly more aware of the reality of
God. As self diminishes within him, God's presence will loom
in a much greater way than in the past. Why is this? Anything
that undermines the self-life promotes humility.

Once the reality of God invades a person's heart, the
natural (and proper) response is to fall on one's face and
worship Him. For instance, when Jesus came walking on the
water "those who were in the boat worshiped him, saying,
'Truly you are the Son of God.'" (Matthew 14:33 NIV) When
the blind man was healed by Jesus in the temple we are told
that the man "worshiped Him." (John 9:38) When the two
Marys met the Resurrected Christ, they "took hold of His
feet and worshiped Him." (Matthew 28:9) All of these who *saw*
the Lord Jesus Christ bowed face down before Him, signify-
ing that they understood they were in the presence of the
Greater One.

But humbling oneself before God is not meant only for
those who have a powerful revelation of Him. Rather, it is
the proper position everyone should take before the Lord in

his heart. Jesus told the woman at the well that the Father actually seeks out people who will worship Him "in spirit and truth." (John 4:23-24) Such devotion is of monumental importance because it involves a person's relationship to the Lord.

In both Hebrew and Greek, the term *worship* conveys the idea of physically prostrating oneself before another. In fact the Greek term gives the sense of a person bowing down in utmost humility to kiss the hand of someone superior.

Many people think that singing hymns and praise songs to God on Sundays is all there is to worship, but it actually has much more to do with a person's conscious subjection to God than it does to singing popular tunes. *True worship only occurs when the person acknowledges who he is in relation to God and who God is in relation to him.* This always requires a great humbling to take place in a person's heart.

The Psalmist brought this truth to light when he said, "Worship the Lord with reverence, and rejoice with trembling. Do homage to the Son, lest He become angry, and you perish in the way..." (Psalm 2:11-12) Such words intimate an unmistakable sense of holy fear and humility in a man who understood his position before God.

Another biblical character who comprehended the true meaning of worship was Job. Nothing will bring out a person's real attitude toward the Lord like trials. When all his earthly possessions were destroyed and his children were killed, "Job arose and tore his robe and shaved his head, and he fell to the ground and worshiped. And he said, 'Naked I came from my mother's womb, and naked I shall return there. The Lord gave and the Lord has taken away. Blessed be the name of the Lord.'" (Job 1:20-21)

Abraham also had a proper attitude toward the Lord. He

had waited 25 years for a son, but when the Lord told him to take a three-day trip to Mount Moriah and sacrifice Isaac, he obeyed without hesitation. After he arrived, he told the young men with him, "Stay here with the donkey, and I and the lad will go yonder; and we will worship and return to you." (Genesis 22:5)

Each of these men illustrates the true meaning of worship. They feared the Lord and maintained their rightful position before Him *in their hearts*. They were so devoted to the Lord that their worship continued even in extremely difficult circumstances. Those who simply "draw near with their words" and whose reverence for Him "consists of tradition learned by rote" (Isaiah 29:13) have no understanding of real worship. Although they may experience a certain vague sense of His presence as they sing hymns and choruses, their revelation of Him will be extremely superficial.

GAINING A TRUE PERSPECTIVE

Many so-called seekers never become intimate with the Lord, never truly humble themselves before Him, and never really worship Him. Pride and other unrepentant sin keeps them at a distance from Him. (Psalm 138:6; Isaiah 59:2) However, what is frightening is that they think they *are* close to God. Pride, like all sin, has the inherent power to deceive a person's heart, thus blinding him to his true spiritual condition. (Obadiah 1:3; Hebrews 3:13) Thus, the very elements at work in the person's life that drive him away from the Lord, simultaneously lead him to believe that he is actually very near to God.

In *At the Altar of Sexual Idolatry*, I wrote about the deceptive power of sin and how the process of overcoming sin brings a person into spiritual reality:

People are prone to overlook their deeply embedded sin because it has an extremely deceptive nature. There exists an interesting correlation between a person's involvement with sin and his awareness of it. The more a person becomes involved in sin, the less he sees it. Sin is a hideous disease that destroys a person's ability to comprehend its existence. It could be compared to a computer virus that has the ability to hide its presence from the user while it systematically destroys the hard drive. Typically, those who are the most entangled in sin are the very ones who cannot see its presence at work inside them. Sin has the ability to mask itself so well that it can actually make the person who deals with it the least, think he is the most spiritual. The Psalmist exposed this person's true heart when he said, "There is no fear of God before his eyes. For in his own eyes he flatters himself too much to detect or hate his sin." (Psalm 36:1b-2 NIV)

On the other hand, the more a person overcomes sin in his life and draws closer to God, the more glaringly his nature of sin stands out. God "dwells in unapproachable light" (I Timothy 6:16) and so consequently, every remnant of selfishness, pride, and sin is going to be exposed to the sincere seeker. The intense, brilliant light of God exposes what is in a person's heart. Those who want to draw near to Him rejoice because of this. They love the Light and so they embrace it, even though it means their true selves will be unmasked. Jesus said, "And this is the judgment, that the light is come into the world, and men loved the darkness rather than the light; for their deeds were evil. For everyone who does evil hates the light, and does not come to the light, lest his deeds should be exposed. But he who practices the truth comes to the light, that his deeds may be manifested as having been wrought in God," (John 3:19-21). [4]

The high-minded person, who does not desire change, remains blissfully ignorant about his true spiritual state. "He flatters himself." Like the self-righteous and self-deceiving Pharisee at the temple, he thinks, prays, and believes the best about himself. Due to his tremendous amount of self-love, he sees himself in the most favorable light.

How different is the believer who is willing to be honest with himself and confesses what is in his heart. As he begins to mature in his walk with God, he starts to recognize sin's ugly tentacles everywhere! It isn't that sin has grown; his blinded eyes have simply been opened to what's been there all along. He now *wants* to see the sin because he desires the Lord to purge it out of him. The person who has been broken by God doesn't need to be convinced of his unworthy condition; his sin is ever before him.

Paul admonished the believer "not to think more highly of himself than he ought to think; but to think so as to have sound judgment." (Romans 12:3) For the most part, humility is simply having the proper perspective about God, about oneself, and about others. William Law said, "Humility does not consist in having a worse opinion of ourselves than we deserve, or in abasing ourselves lower than we really are; but as all virtue is founded in truth, so humility is founded in a true and just sense of our weakness, misery, and sin. He that rightly feels and lives in this sense of his condition, lives in humility." [5] Matthew Henry expressed the same sentiment: "Humility is an estimate of ourselves as we are. It is a willingness to be known, and talked

> **Coming into a true knowledge about one's self is very humbling.**

of, and treated just according to truth. It is a view of ourselves as lost, poor, and wandering creatures." [6]

Coming into a true knowledge about one's self is very humbling. The wonderful benefit of it is that as the believer becomes smaller in his own mind, God becomes bigger. As the person's awareness grows about the limitations of his own goodness—thereby diminishing the blinding effects of self-righteousness—the way is opened for him to see the infinite goodness of God. As he sees how selfish he is, he becomes more cognizant of the Lord's selflessness. When he recognizes how little love he actually has for others, his eyes will be opened to the Lord's overwhelming love.

As a person becomes little in his own sight, he will have a much greater reality of the Lord in his life. An entire realm that had previously been unknown to him will open up. His spirit will become sensitized to the kingdom of God. The Scriptures will come alive and prayer will be revitalized. Then this growing awareness will infect every other area of his life. Love, joy, and peace will all begin to spring forth within. (Galatians 5:22) The more real God's presence becomes to him, the more fulfilled he will be. In essence, God infuses his being with abundant life. A cup that runs over truly awaits every believer who humbles himself before the Lord.

A NEW PERSPECTIVE ON OTHERS

The end result of humbling oneself before the Lord is that one's perception of other people will greatly change. Once self has been dethroned, a believer is able to see others in a completely new light: people become more important as they are seen through the eyes of God's love.

Peter showed the connection between one's relation to God and others when he said, "...all of you, clothe yourselves with humility toward one another, for God is opposed to the proud, but gives grace to the humble. Humble yourselves, therefore, under the mighty hand of God, that He may exalt you at the proper time." (I Peter 5:5-6)

The type of clothing a person wears physically often identifies what he is like. For instance, a Hell's Angel wears his "colors," the patch on his jacket that represents violence and viciousness. A businessman flaunts his success by wearing an expensive suit. A seductive woman attracts stares with a tight blouse and a short skirt. It is very important to these individuals that their outfits properly represent the image they wish to project to others. And believe it or not, pride is the motivating factor behind all of this.

However, Peter exhorts Christians to accentuate their inner man with lowliness. This means that they should convey this impression to the people they live and work with. Their humble demeanor should be as obvious as the coat they are wearing. In biblical times, the servant wore certain attire that identified him as such. It was clear to everyone around him that he was someone's servant, a member of the lowest class in society. Peter's audience clearly understood the implications of his statement.

Jesus, who frequently spoke in parables to convey truth, illustrated this spiritual principle by acting it out before His disciples. John said that He "rose from supper, and laid aside His garments; and taking a towel, He girded Himself about. Then He poured water into the basin, and began to wash the disciples' feet, and to

> A Hell's Angel wears his "colors," the patch on his jacket that represents violence and viciousness.

If you know these things, you are blessed if you do them. wipe them with the towel with which He was girded." (John 13:4-5) By "girding Himself" with a towel and performing the task of a servant, He showed His disciples what He expected from their lives: they were to follow in His steps by loving and serving others.

He then explained His actions. "You call Me Teacher and Lord; and you are right, for so I am. If I then, the Lord and the Teacher, washed your feet, you also ought to wash one another's feet. For I gave you an example that you also should do as I did to you. Truly, truly, I say to you, a slave is not greater than his master; neither is one who is sent greater than the one who sent him. If you know these things, you are blessed if you do them." (John 13:13-17) Jesus did not institute a new sacrament. He simply showed them that a true servant of God must possess a lowly mentality.

Paul used vivid terms to address the believer's relationships with others: "And so, as those who have been chosen of God, holy and beloved, put on a heart of compassion, kindness, humility, gentleness and patience; bearing with one another, and forgiving each other, whoever has a complaint against anyone; just as the Lord forgave you, so also should you. And beyond all these things put on love, which is the perfect bond of unity." (Colossians 3:12-14)

While we all have areas of pride within the framework of our characters, we must still strive to humble ourselves before God and man. Here are a few things we can do to put on humility:

- We can acknowledge our sin to the Lord.
- We can worship Him with true reverence.
- We can treat others with kindness, patience and gentleness.

- We can be quick to forgive the wrongs of others.
- We can show compassion toward them, doing our best to meet their needs.

In other words, humility should not simply be some vague concept but a very real part of the believer's daily life.

Dear Lord, I realize that I am too large in my own mind. I repent! Please humble me so that I can better see You. Bring me out of any self-deception pride or sin has created. Help me to acquire the proper perspective of myself in relation to You and others. Make me fear you! Give me a servant's heart. Purify me, O Lord, so that I might live humbly before You and others.
Amen.

"I used to think that God's gifts were on shelves one above the other and that the taller we grew in Christian character, the more easily we should reach them. I find now that God's gifts are on shelves one beneath the other and that it is not a question of growing taller, but of stooping lower and that we have to go down, always down to get His best ones. In Christian service the branches that bear the most fruit hang the lowest." [1]

F.B. Meyer

"Our humility must not only be a lowly estimate of ourselves, but it must be a practical stripping off of distinctions and prerogatives and an identifying of ourselves with the lowliest. It must lead to service. That service must have for its end our brother's cleansing. The humble mind thinks not of its claims on others, but of its duties to them." [2]

Alexander MacClaren

ten

SERVING OTHERS

CONVENTIONAL WISDOM EQUATES
humility with human modesty. In the world's
eyes, humble people are those who are mild-
mannered by nature. However, according to God's standard,
sometimes outwardly modest people are the most selfish and
prideful folks around. The truth is that godly humility has
nothing to do with a person's natural disposition. For example, He took two tough guys and radically transformed
them by the power of the Holy Spirit: loud-mouthed, self-
assertive Peter and Paul, who was once "a violent aggres-
sor." Both men were brought low, walked in humility, and
were true bondservants of Jesus Christ.

A person comes into humility as his awareness of, concern for and devotion to God and others increase. Paul himself gives what is perhaps the best definition of humility:
"Do nothing from selfishness or empty conceit, but with
humility of mind let each of you regard one another as more
important than himself; do not merely look out for your own
personal interests, but also for the interests of others."
(Philippians 2:3-4)

One essential aspect of humility is living in the constant
awareness of the importance of other people. As a believer

> As self-consciousness decreases, he becomes increasingly aware of "the interests of others."

becomes involved in the lives of others, he becomes less consumed with himself. Conversely, the prideful person is preoccupied with self. His thinking almost always revolves around his own opinions, desires, and needs. Socially, he really is only concerned with himself and his own family. There is very little room left for anybody else because he is so huge in his own mind. Rather than serve others, he seeks to be served.

On the other hand, the humble believer matures out of that selfish thinking and becomes interested in other people. As self-consciousness decreases, he becomes increasingly aware of "the interests of others." Their lives take up a greater part of his consciousness, and he becomes smaller in his own mind. Humility is living with a great concern about the well-being of others and allowing their interests, needs, struggles, dreams, and fears to play a big part in one's own life. Every Christian is expected to bear others' burdens in order to "fulfill the law of Christ." (Galatians 6:2)

Paul exhorted Christians to "be devoted to one another in brotherly love; give preference to one another in honor... contributing to the needs of the saints, practicing hospitality. Bless those who persecute you; bless and curse not. Rejoice with those who rejoice, and weep with those who weep. Be of the same mind toward one another; do not be haughty in mind, but associate with the lowly. Do not be wise in your own estimation." (Romans 12:10-16)

This is a fuller definition of humility and describes what should characterize the normal Christian life. Anyone who has the Spirit of Christ living within him will have an inner compulsion to help those around him who are in need. For instance, take a look at what Jesus did in a two-day period as recorded in Matthew chapters 5-9:

DAY ONE:
- He preached the Sermon on the Mount;
- Healed a leper;
- Healed the centurion's servant;
- Healed Peter's mother-in-law;
- Healed and delivered many people that evening;
- Got in a boat to cross the Sea of Galilee and fell asleep;
- Dispelled a storm that assaulted the boat;

DAY TWO:
- Cast the demons out of two men on the other side;
- Crossed the lake back to Capernaum;
- Healed a paralytic;
- Debated the Pharisees;
- Ate dinner with Matthew and his friends;
- Healed the woman with the issue of blood;
- Raised Jairus' daughter from the dead;
- Healed two blind men; and finally,
- Cast a devil out of another man.

I am grateful that Matthew featured this snap-shot of the daily life of the Savior, rather than simply recording all the major events that occurred during His three-plus years of ministry. This glimpse into His everyday life reveals His constant concern for the lives of other people. According to His mission statement, He "came to serve, not to be served." (Matthew 20:28)

According to His mission statement, He "came to serve, not to be served."

True followers of Christ adopt this

same mentality because Christ lives within them.* When they see need, they are compelled to meet that need. Christian servants aren't people that one orders around, like a rich person treats a butler. They are those who—under the rule of their Master—live their lives to meet the *needs* of others. In a sense they are subservient to those needs.

Paul is a prime example of this posture of heart. He continually identified himself as a bondservant, spending his 30 years of ministry serving and meeting the spiritual needs of his Gentile converts. What he endured for their sakes is absolutely phenomenal. Thus, the things he might have desired for himself—comfort, safety, pleasure, prosperity, and so on—all took a backseat to the great call he had received from Jesus Christ to take them the Gospel. There wasn't anything—not even martyrdom—that he wouldn't go through toward that end.

The book of First Thessalonians reveals Paul's great love for people. Read some of the things he said to this congregation who meant so very much to him:

- We were all the more eager with great desire to see your face (2:17);
- We wanted to come to you—I, Paul, more than once—and yet Satan thwarted us (2:18);
- For who is our hope or joy or crown of exultation? Is it not even you? (2:19);
- For you are our glory and joy (2:20);
- When we could endure it no longer (3:1);
- When I could endure it no longer, I also sent to find out about your faith, for fear that the tempter might

---

* The religious person might go to church and swear off obvious, outward sins, but if he has not had a true conversion, he will lack that inner compulsion to meet the needs of others. James asserted that saving faith was proven by its deeds of mercy. (James 2:13-26)

have tempted you (3:5);
- We also long to see you (3:6);
- Now we really live, if you stand firm in the Lord (3:8);
- All the joy with which we rejoice before our God on your account (3:9); and lastly,
- We night and day keep praying most earnestly that we may see your face, and may complete what is lacking in your faith (3:10).

Paul's great devotion to these people is very obvious. His entire life revolved around their well-being. His obvious burden for lost souls drove him on relentlessly. People were lost in darkness and going to hell and *he cared deeply*. This is the mindset that every believer should have.

"SELF" SERVING

How different is the mentality that many have today. The story of a young man named Keith (a pseudonym) comes to mind. He entered the Pure Life Ministries residential program because of his struggle with homosexuality. He quickly got saved and went on to find much freedom from his sexual sin. He felt called into ministry and eventually entered Bible school with the staff's blessing. We were all very happy for him when he graduated two years later and were delighted to hire him when he asked for a job.

However, when he arrived it quickly became apparent that he had lost some of the servanthood principles we had instilled into him. We had taught him that the primary purpose of ministry is to help other people. Somehow, by the time he had graduated, his primary focus was on building a ministerial career that revolved around him. It seemed clear that he wanted to become somebody great and ministry was his ticket to greatness.

This attitude was revealed in one particular conversation I had with him several months after he had returned to work for us. Keith was still struggling with habitual masturbation. However, he told me he had a dream the night before in which the Lord told him that He wanted to use him in a great way, but that He was unable to because of his masturbation habit. I knew the dream was not from the Lord because masturbation was merely a symptom of a much deeper issue.

"Keith, the Lord *does* want to use you, but masturbation isn't the problem; you are the problem!" I exclaimed. "Masturbation, anger, bitterness and the other things you struggle with are the out-workings of the flesh. To put it in the simplest terms: the problem is that you are still very much full of self. As long as you are full of yourself, God will be very limited in what He can do through you."

"The other thing you need to know is that your understanding of serving the Lord is out of whack," I went on to tell him. "Keith, ministry should not revolve around the idea of YOU being used in a great way. Such thinking is foreign to the kingdom of God. Your perspective is that you are going to do great exploits for the Lord. Your whole motivation for service centers around you: what you will get out of it, how people will look up to you, how great you will appear to others."

"Greatness in the kingdom of God revolves around the Lord, not the worker," I concluded. "The Lord is the One with the magnanimous heart. He is the Person who possesses an enormous love for others. He is the One who is willing to do anything in His power to help them. Our part is to empty ourselves so that we might be a channel for His love and power."

I could tell he did not like my little speech very much. He politely listened and left the room. A couple of weeks later, he told me that God had called him to work as a missionary in another country. I knew what that meant: he had rejected the concept of servanthood. He was determined to make a name for himself.

> I could tell he did not like my little speech very much. He politely listened and left the room.

It did not come as a huge surprise when I found out later that he failed to make his big "splash" in the kingdom of God and had indeed backslid after leaving Pure Life Ministries. I knew that God had sent him to us so that we could teach him how to serve others. Unfortunately, this concept did not fit in with his agenda.

YOUR SPECIAL CALLING

Every believer is called to serve, whether it is in official ministry or not. In fact, ordinary lay people who are only interested in pleasing Jesus do some of the most wonderful, Spirit-filled work that takes place. The following story illustrates the fact that any believer can help others:

Richard Sobotka is 23 years old. He suffered from Reye's syndrome at age 9. This illness causes swelling of the brain tissue, leaving irreversible damage. Its effect on Richard has been loss of speech abilities and some motor skills. He breathes through a tracheotomy tube. These might seem to be great disabilities, but Richard has learned to serve the Lord with what he has.

Last fall, he decided to collect the fallen walnuts

from the grove on his parents' property. He could sell the walnuts and earn some money.

Richard spent one full week gathering walnuts. This was a great task, as his disabilities prevent stooping.

He sat on the ground, palming the walnut with two operational fingers, then dropping them into bags. His harvest was impressive: 270 pounds of walnuts were collected in 16 to 20 tow sacks. Richard took the walnuts to a local huller and received $21.60 for his labors.

Instead of keeping the money for personal use, he decided to send it to Missionaries Bill and Judy Kirsch in South Africa. Bill wrote that the offering "may well be the most generous offering we have ever received . . . In many ways, Richard is an example to us all. He models the kind of servanthood and self-sacrifice that pleases Christ and that we so often in our abundance and health neglect." [3]

When God calls a believer to eternal life, He also calls him into His service. The Church is called the Body of Christ. Every member has his place. The Lord has perfectly crafted a ministry that is suited to the temperament, abilities and faith of each Christian. A.B. Simpson said this:

There is something you can do that no one else can do; there is someone you can reach that no one else can reach. Your talent may consist of natural ability, social influence, financial resources, position in the church or the world, or special opportunities brought to you in connection with your life work. It is the sum of all the possibilities of usefulness in your life. God expects you to make the most of it for Him and others and is going to call you to account at the coming of Christ for the use you have made of your life. [4]

As servants of Christ, it is our responsibility to discover God's will for us. Richard didn't have much to offer, but he gave all he had. The possibilities of getting involved in the needs of others are limitless. Nursing homes are always looking for volunteers to help the elderly who have often been forgotten and abandoned by family and friends. What a wonderful place to repay God for all the mercy He has shown. Jail ministries need men who will take an interest in those behind bars. Soup kitchens want people who will serve unselfishly. Para-church ministries could do with volunteers to help out in a variety of ways. Elderly neighbors can always use a hand doing laundry, driving them to the store, mowing their lawn, and so on.

Most pastors are inundated with pastoral obligations and various problems concerning members of their congregation and have very few people willing to give of their time. A helpful Christian can ask his pastor if there is some work that needs to be done around the church occasionally. A person with mechanical skills can offer to help with ministry vehicles or maintenance work. Those with administrative abilities can offer to do typing, prepare a monthly newsletter, arrange visitation, or a number of other things. Friendly people can act as greeters on Sunday mornings, visit new members, or teach Sunday school. Any of these deeds of mercy are just as important as preaching and teaching in the kingdom of God.

There is no shortage of needs to be filled. God has a will for everyone's life. He has some task that is specially suited for each person. The important thing for the believer is to become involved helping others in whatever way he can. This is the mindset of the kingdom of heaven. What could be more gratifying on earth than doing the will of God? Those who are not fulfilling the call God has placed on their lives will never know the joy they are missing.

❧

Dear Lord, please convict me of my lack of concern for others. Put a burden on my heart that will press upon me day after day until I respond. Help me to see the needs of others and give me the grace to do my part to fill those needs. Make your will known to me and I promise that I will obey your call.
Thank you, Lord.
Amen.

"Most of us value the quality in a person which, when communicated to us, says, 'You are certainly my equal and, in many ways, my better.'" [1]
Anonymous

"People are by nature selfish, and it is the design of religion to make them benevolent. They seek their own interests by nature, and the gospel would teach them to regard the welfare of others. If we are truly under the influence of religion, there is not a member of the church in whom we should not feel an interest, and whose welfare we should not strive to promote as far as we have opportunity." [2]
Albert Barnes

eleven

COMING DOWN AND GOING UNDER

ALL SINCERE BELIEVERS RUTHLESSLY GO after everything in their lives that are displeasing to God. They earnestly desire to be pure in heart. (Matthew 5:7) They realize that earth is a temporary testing ground and that every thought, word, and action will one day be judged. What they have allowed God to do within them and through them will determine the quality and measure of reward they will possess for endless ages. These saints understand that the quality and measure of their rewards will be based primarily upon the degree to which they have allowed God to conquer them inside and mold them into the likeness of Jesus Christ. (Romans 8:29) David's prayer is continually on their lips: "Search me, O God, and know my heart: try me, and know my thoughts: and see if there be any wicked way in me, and lead me in the way everlasting." (Psalm 139:23-24 KJV)

How different is the mindset of those who live only for today. The Bible calls them fools: those who do not think things through and make decisions with only the immediate dividends in mind. Surely the things Scripture says about them are certainly true:

- Fools despise wisdom and instruction. (Proverbs 1:7)

- The way of a fool is right in his own eyes. (Proverbs 12:15)
- Fools mock at sin. (Proverbs 14:9)
- A fool is arrogant and careless. (Proverbs 14:16)
- A fool rejects his father's discipline. (Proverbs 15:5)
- The mind of fools is in the house of pleasure. (Ecclesiastes 7:4)

These passages serve as a good reminder of the importance of allowing the Holy Spirit to accomplish His work within the heart. Much is at stake and it is an undeniable fact that one of man's greatest needs is to be humbled. Up to this point, much of this book has dealt with the dual subject of pride/humility from a theoretical standpoint. I will now present concrete steps which the reader can take to fully cooperate with God's work in his life.

ADDRESSING PRIDE

If you desire to walk in humility you must first determine which forms of pride are at work in your heart. Ask yourself the following questions:
- "Are there ways in which I act superior to others?"
- "Do I look for and attempt to garner the admiration of others?"
- "Am I touchy and defensive?"
- "Do I tend to come across as a know-it-all?"
- "Am I rebellious to my leaders?"
- "Do I resist God's authority in my life?"
- "Do I attempt to get glory for what God has done in me or through me?"

It would be wise to lay them out before the Lord and ask Him to reveal those areas of your heart sullied by pride.

Most of us—if we are honest with ourselves—will easily identify several types of pride at work in our hearts. Without getting discouraged or wallowing in self-pity, take each one to the Lord individually. Acknowledge it and ask Him to forgive you for all the ways it has caused you to mistreat Him and other people. You might even recollect some things you have thought, said, or done and will want to go to those you have sinned against to ask their forgiveness.

Having repented, it is now time to take action against each type of pride you struggle with. Part of this will be to counteract your natural prideful tendencies by putting off pride and putting on humility. (Ephesians 4:22-24)

For instance, a haughty person needs to do things that will bring him down (in his mind) to the level of others. If he is arrogant about his accomplishments, he should develop the habit of praising other people for their achievements. Transferring the focus from self to others in this way could do much to defeat a superior attitude. Also, develop the habit of acknowledging your own faults to those around you. For instance, Bill Johnson could help himself by really considering why it is that people like Jim the custodian far more than they like him.

The vain person needs to overcome his tendency to look for approval from others. Although vanity is not the form of pride I typically struggle with, I see all too clearly my propensity to present myself in the most favorable light. To combat this natural inclination, I will often purposely do things which place me in an unfavorable light. For instance, if I am going shopping with my wife, rather than wearing "business casual" attire, I might put on the muddy jeans and boots I wear during my morning prayer walks in the woods. Perhaps this seems silly and unnecessary, but it is one little thing I can do to go against the natural "flow" of my pride. Trust me; this kind of behavior does wonders to squelch the vain person's need to be highly regarded.

Someone who struggles with being overly protective would approach things differently. He must let down his guard, realizing that it is okay to be seen as being less than perfect. In fact, it is a liberating experience that will help him to become a warmer and more loving person. As he learns to make himself more vulnerable to others, he will find that his towering, self-protective walls will come tumbling down. Those walls represent a fear of man that can only be replaced as a greater concern for others grows. The aged apostle of love said, "There is no fear in love; but perfect love casts out fear, because fear involves punishment, and the one who fears is not perfected in love." (I John 4:18) In other words, the more involved you become in the lives of others, the less of a hold fear will have within you.

An individual who is rebellious or tends to be unapproachable must deal mercilessly with his pride because confrontation plays such a vital role in the kingdom of God. It would be wise for him to approach his spiritual leaders and/or those closest to him, acknowledging these inclinations and inviting their input into his life. The wise words of Solomon express why this is so vital: "He who corrects a scoffer gets dishonor for himself, and he who reproves a wicked man gets insults for himself. Do not reprove a scoffer, lest he hate you, reprove a wise man, and he will love you." (Proverbs 9:7-8)

A highly accomplished person typically struggles with know-it-all pride in his areas of interest; he can be quite smug about his level of knowledge. One good way for him to battle this attitude is to purposely go to others seeking advice or information on different subjects. This can be extremely difficult (and humbling) for him because he is so talented. However, it will do him a tremendous amount of good and will be a blessing to others at the same time.

> Going against the natural flow of pride in one's life helps tremendously to bring it under control.

Spiritual pride requires a great deal of deep repentance before God. Someone who deals with this form of pride tends to exaggerate his spirituality. It would be prudent of him to ask the Lord to bring him into a greater sight of how much he is lacking spiritually. He cannot make himself poor in spirit, but he can seek God to do it.

Going against the natural flow of pride in one's life helps tremendously to bring it under control. One word of caution should be mentioned here. As you begin to see different kinds of pride in your own life, you will inevitably become more aware of them in those around you. You must guard yourself against this tendency and avoid being critical toward them. Rather than pointing out their errors, look for ways to serve them.

WAYS TO HUMBLE ONESELF

Besides addressing particular attitudes of pride you may possess, there are other practical things you can do to humble yourself with others.

First of all, you must change the way you view those around you. Rather than seeing them as rivals to compete with, consider them as objects of your love, respect, and affection. God loves them and sent His Son to die on a cross that they might have life. They ought to have the best you have to offer. One morning in prayer, during the early years of my ministry, the Lord impressed upon my heart that the

> **This revelation really changed the way I viewed them from then on.**

men who came into our residential program were His special guests and deserved to be treated as such. This revelation really changed the way I viewed them from then on.

Second, recognize how the spirit of this world has affected your perspectives of life and the way you view yourself and others. Consider the words of William Law, who wrote this several centuries before television, radio, and computers began to shape modern thinking:

> The devil is called in Scripture the prince of this world, because he has great power in it, because many of its rules and principles are invented by this evil spirit, the father of all lies and falsehoods, to separate us from God, and prevent our return to happiness.
>
> Now, according to the spirit and vogue of this world, whose corrupt air we have all breathed... we dare not attempt to be eminent in the sight of God and holy angels, for fear of being little in the eyes of the world.
>
> From this quarter arises the greatest difficulty of humility, because it cannot subsist in any mind, but so far as it is dead to the world, and has parted with all desires of enjoying its greatness and honors. So that in order to be truly humble, you must unlearn all those notions which you have been all your life learning from this corrupt spirit of the world. You can make no stand against the assaults of pride, the meek affections of humility can have no place in your soul, till you stop the power of the world over you, and resolve against a blind obedience to its laws. [3]

Next, change the way you interact with others. One of the things we teach the men who come into our residential program is summed up with the phrase, "going under others." When there is a conflict between two people, in a very real sense each person is attempting to go over the top of the other with his argument or wish. To a large extent, the humble person will allow the other to have his way. For instance, when the two hold differing opinions over some controversial subject, the humble man will graciously allow the other individual to express his viewpoint without feeling a need to argue. Solomon said, "The beginning of strife is like letting out water, so abandon the quarrel before it breaks out." (Proverbs 17:14) He also said, "A gentle answer turns away wrath, but a harsh word stirs up anger." (Proverbs 15:1) Allowing the other person to express his viewpoints unchallenged does not mean that you agree with what he says; it simply means that you have the wisdom to realize that nothing good will come out of further discussion. A good way to handle this kind of dispute is to smile and say, "I see your point" and tactfully change the subject.

If you feel that there is the possibility you can exchange ideas with the person, you might say, "Yes, I think I can understand why you feel that way. I could very well be wrong, but the way I see it is..." Express your opinion in gentle terms and watch his reaction. If you get the sense that he is digging in his heels, revert to the approach mentioned above. Hold your peace and avoid unnecessary conflict.

This concept of "going under" also involves letting others have their way, whenever it is in your power to do so. If someone wants the last piece of pie, let him have it. If someone cuts in line in front of you, don't make an issue of it. If you don't want to go out to dinner but your spouse does, go

> One of the marks of true Christianity is yielding one's will to that of another.

out to dinner! One of the marks of true Christianity is yielding one's will to that of another. It goes without saying that this does not hold true in the case of a parent disciplining his child, a teacher insisting that a student complete his studies, a pastor reproving a false teacher, and so on.

It is also important to be quick to say that you are wrong. If you get in a disagreement with someone, apologize for your fault in the matter—whether or not they are willing to do the same. You will be able to walk away from the situation knowing that you have pleased God.

One of the difficulties people have with saying that they are wrong is that they are so accustomed to thinking they are right about everything. However, even if that person was not wrong in what he said to the other individual, chances are the attitude in his heart was wrong. The Pharisees were "right" in many of the things they taught but how terribly wrong they were in their self-righteous disdain for others. Be quick to apologize to others and ask forgiveness, and be slow to defend yourself. There are Christians who are so proud that they have literally gone years without admitting fault about anything!

Always be ready to give credit where it is due. Take note of the good that people do. Let them know that you appreciate their efforts. Get into the habit of promoting others, rather than yourself. One minister said, "If we love others the way Jesus does we will rejoice so much in seeing them achieve and enjoy the position of being first that we will hardly notice that in our efforts to help them we turned up last." [4] Or to put it into the words of the Savior: "And just as you want people to treat you, treat them in the same way." (Luke 6:31)

Lastly, get involved in the lives of other people. Show that you care about them. In the last chapter we explored different ways you can help to meet the needs of others. Not only should you do acts of kindness, but you should also express an attitude of concern for them. For instance, engage them in conversations about themselves:

"What do you do for a living? How are things going on your job?"

"Do you have children? Tell me about them."

"Where did you grow up? Does your family still live there?"

"What part of town do you live in? Do you like it there?"

People love to talk about themselves. Questions like these will help them to open up to you and see that you care about them. As you involve yourself in the lives of others, you will find God's love increasing within your heart toward them. It may seem mechanical and contrived initially, but don't let that hinder you! The Lord is instilling His great love for others inside you. Do everything you possibly can to cooperate with His efforts. Every person you come in contact with is extremely important to God. It would please Him greatly if you too took an interest in their lives.

&

Dear Lord, you see the different types of pride in my life. I acknowledge the fact that they are at work within me. Lord, please help me to overcome each of them. They make me ugly and limit my ability to properly represent you to others. Holy Spirit, I invite you to convict me every time I act or think that way in the future. Lord, I repent of it and I promise that I will do the best I can to quit coming across that way to others. Please root it all out of me. I ask you to humble me and help me to see how little I truly am. Thank you for helping me. Amen.

"Humility is so amiable a quality, that it forces our esteem wherever we meet with it. There is no possibility of despising the lowest person that has it or of esteeming the greatest man that lacks it." [1]

William Law

twelve

IRRESISTIBLE SAINTS

THUS FAR WE HAVE EXAMINED THE subject of God's abhorrence of pride and His admiration for humility. The premise of this book—that I have endeavored to establish through Scripture—is that pride exacts a terrible price upon one's life, while humility brings God's favor and blessings.

In a culture where it is so easy to make big bucks in a short period of time and in a religious environment in which ministers are rewarded according to their natural abilities and charisma, God's blessings are taken for granted quite often. If a person can compensate himself, why should he go the narrow path of brokenness and humility? The answer is that sincere Christians want to please God and live with an eternal perspective. One day those who have faked their way to the top will be exposed for what they really are, while those who have humbled themselves before God will be openly rewarded.

I realize that I have not personally traveled very far on this path toward humility. However, I can see it and I'm determined to stay on it regardless of the temporary cost involved at times. I want my life to be pleasing to the Lord and—after all He has done for me—I don't want to stand before Him with a legacy of pride and selfishness.

Having said that, I will conclude this book with the stories of three renowned saints whose lives testify to the fact that God "gives grace to the humble." It is easy to see how the Lord honored and greatly used them in His kingdom. Their biographies are well known, so I will primarily focus on statements and anecdotes that reveal their characters.

TREMBLING BEFORE GOD

"For who has despised the day of small things?" (Zechariah 4:10)

You would think that one of the major denominations would have birthed the modern-day missionary movement—that its pioneer would have had hands laid on him in one of the grand cathedrals and would have been the subject of a glorious farewell celebration. However, it was modest means that inaugurated this monumental segment of church history.

As a young Christian, William Carey and a couple of friends formed a "mission society" to explore the idea of taking the gospel to India. However, when they shared their idea at the local ministers' meeting, they were ridiculed to scorn. Undaunted, young William began making plans to go to India. Upon hearing of his plans, his father wrote him a scathing letter and rebuked him for such a fool-hearty pursuit. Worse than that, his wife refused to go or allow their children to go. William responded to his wife in a letter dated May 6, 1793: "If I had all the world, I would freely give it all to have you and my children with me, but the

His wife refused to go or allow their children to go.

sense of duty is so strong as to overpower all other consider-
ations. I cannot turn back without guilt on my soul." Dorothy finally relented, and the small party boarded a ship that
arrived in Calcutta six months later.

However, the modern missionary movement did not
begin without much opposition. Within a few months, their
money was gone. Just when it seemed that it couldn't get any
worse—living in a strange country where they knew nobody—Mrs. Carey and their son both became seriously ill.
Nevertheless, God intervened and before long they were
healthy and were able to secure a modest income. Unfortunately, Dorothy's heart was not united with William in the
venture. Rather than seeing it as a marvelous opportunity to
serve God and bring Christianity to a nation steeped in spiritual darkness, all she could see were the hardships. When
their youngest son died, she went over the edge emotionally.
Carey's first seven years in India were extremely difficult, but
this period was the crucible where his faith was tested and
his self-life crushed.

Eventually others joined them from England. Before long,
the little band of missionaries was busily printing portions
of Scripture in the local language. During the course of the
next 30 years, William translated all or parts of the Bible into
25 different Indian languages and dialects. In 1825 he wrote,
"The New Testament will soon be printed in thirty-four languages, and the Old Testament in eight, besides versions in
three varieties of the Hindustani New Testament." Not only
this, but he opened many schools to train children and a Bible
college that would send out Christian ministers for many years
to come.

Although his beginnings were humble, God mightily used
his life to open up an entire region of the world that had
been sealed shut to the Gospel. However, as his life began to

come to an end, he directed all the praise to the Lord for every accomplishment. George Gogerly, one of his contemporaries, tells of visiting the old missionary days before his death.

"He was seated near his desk in the study, dressed in his usual neat attire. His eyes were closed and his hands clasped together... (His appearance) filled me with a kind of awe, for he seemed as one listening to his Master's summons, and ready to go. I sat there for about half an hour without a word, for I feared to break that silence, and to call back to earth the spirit that seemed almost in heaven. At last, however, I spoke, and well do I remember the very words that passed between us.

"'Dear friend,' said Gogerly, 'you seem to be standing on the very border of eternity. Do not think it wrong then that I ask your thoughts and feelings.'

"The question roused Dr. Carey. Slowly he opened his eyes, and then with a feeble though earnest voice he answered: 'I know in whom I have believed, and am persuaded that He is able to keep that which I have committed unto Him against that day. But when I think I am about to appear in God's holy presence, and I remember all my sins, I tremble.'" [2] He died two days later.

A few days before this visit, as his health seemed to be deteriorating beyond all hope of recovery, another friend asked if he had any preference as to the passage of Scripture used for his funeral sermon. He replied, "Oh, I feel that such a poor, sinful creature is unworthy to have anything said about him; but if a funeral sermon must be preached, let it be from the words, 'Have mercy upon me, O God, according to Thy lovingkindness; according unto the multitude of Thy tender mercies blot out my transgressions.'"

At his request, cut into his gravestone were the following words:

William Carey
Born August 17th, 1761 Died June 9th, 1834
A wretched, poor, and helpless worm
On Thy kind arms I fall.

DEPENDENT LIKE A CHILD

"Whoever then humbles himself as this child, he is the greatest in
the kingdom of heaven. And whoever receives one such child in
My name receives Me." (Matthew 18:4-5)

After several years in ministry in England, George Mueller began to feel a great burden over the terrible plight of the orphans of his day. "His heart went out to the many ragged children running wild in the streets." He decided he must do something and rented a house for 26 little girls in a residential area of Bristol. Over the course of the next several years, three more homes were also rented, allowing room for 100 more boys and girls.

The remarkable aspect of Mueller's ministry was that he never made his needs known to others. He simply asked God to burden people to give to his work. This determination to trust God alone would be tested many times. The following story is fairly typical of the way he depended upon the Lord for every need.

One morning the plates and cups and bowls on the table were empty. There was no food in the larder, and no money to buy food. The children were standing waiting for their morning meal, when

Mueller said, "Children, you know we must be in time for school." Lifting his hand he said, "Dear Father, we thank Thee for what Thou art going to give us to eat." There was a knock on the door. The baker stood there, and said, "Mr. Mueller, I couldn't sleep last night. Somehow I felt you didn't have bread for breakfast and the Lord wanted me to send you some. So I got up at 2 a.m. and baked some fresh bread, and have brought it." Mueller thanked the man. No sooner had this transpired when there was a second knock at the door. It was the milkman. He announced that his milk cart had broken down right in front of the Orphanage, and he would like to give the children his cans of fresh milk so he could empty his wagon and repair it. No wonder, years later, when Mueller was to travel the world as an evangelist, he would be heralded as "the man who gets things from God!" [3]

In 1846, Mr. Mueller felt led to move the kids out of the tight confines of his neighborhood. Moreover, applications of other needy children continued to pour into his office. He had to do more! He began to seek God about the possibility of constructing a building. Three years later the first Orphan House was completed, with room for 335 children!

No sooner had this home been completed than George set out to build another one. There were still so many hurting children, and by God's grace he would help as many as he could. Once again, he began to pray. He was not concerned about whether or not the Lord would provide, but about his motives. "Would building another Orphan House cause me to be lifted up in pride?" he asked himself. "There is danger of this... One tenth of service with which He has entrusted me would be enough to puff me up with pride. I

IRRESISTIBLE SAINTS
cannot say that the Lord has kept me humble. But I can say that He has given me a hearty desire to give to Him all the glory... I do not see, therefore, that fear of pride should keep me from going forward in this work.

> "If I was left to myself, I would fall prey to (Satan) at once."

Rather, I ask the Lord to give me a humble attitude." [4]

Within nine years of building the first home, he had opened two more. This allowed for the care of over 1,200 orphans. By 1870, he had five orphanages operating with over 2,000 children being cared for.

He once stated, "If I was left to myself, I would fall prey to (Satan) at once. Pride, unbelief, or other sins would be my ruin and lead me to bring disgrace upon the name of Jesus. No one should admire me, be astonished at my faith, or think of me as if I were an amazing person. No, I am as weak as ever. I need to be upheld in faith and every other grace." [5]

Mr. Mueller died in 1898. Not long before this, a friend said to him, "When God calls you home, Mr. Mueller, it will be like a ship going into harbor in full sail."

"Oh, no, he said, "it is poor George Mueller, who needs daily to pray, 'Uphold my goings... that my footsteps slip not.'" [6]

LITTLE IN HIS OWN EYES

"My grace is sufficient for you, for my power is made perfect in weakness."
(II Corinthians 12:9 NIV)

Hudson Taylor, the man of small stature who had a big heart for China, was born in England in 1832. As a young man, he sensed the call of God on his life to the mis-

159

sion field and entered medical school. Little did he know then how he would be severely tested in the years ahead. While still in London he came down with a life-threatening disease and spent months so sick that he could barely manage to get out of bed. He finally got better and booked passage on a ship headed to China.

Taylor arrived in Shanghai in 1854 and soon began making forays into the countryside to preach the gospel. The lack of response from the people brought him to conclude that the problem was that he was dressed so strangely to them. Much to the amusement of the other missionaries, the earnest young man exchanged his European attire for that of the local people.

On one evangelistic trip Taylor and his traveling companion were warned not to enter the city they were approaching, as the soldiers there would most surely kill them. They would not be dissuaded because they felt that God sent them there. He tells what happened as they approached the city:

> Long before we reached the gate, however, a tall powerful man, made ten-fold fiercer by partial intoxication, let us know that all the militia were not so peaceably inclined, by seizing Mr. Burdon by the shoulders. My companion endeavored to shake him off. I turned to see what was the matter, and at once we were surrounded by a dozen or more brutal men, who hurried us on to the city at a fearful pace.
>
> My bag began to feel very heavy, and I could not change hands to relieve myself. I was soon in a profuse perspiration, and was scarcely able to keep pace with them. We demanded to be taken before the chief magistrate, but were told that they knew where to take us, and what to do with such persons as we were,

with the most insulting epithets. The man who first seized Mr. Burdon soon afterward left him for me, and became my principal tormentor; for I was neither so tall nor so strong as my friend, and was therefore less able to resist him. He all but knocked me down again and again, seized me by the hair, took hold of my collar so as to almost choke me, and grasped my arms and shoulders, making them black and blue. Had this treatment continued much longer, I must have fainted. [7]

At last they were taken to a magistrate's office and were then treated with more respect. The magistrate felt so badly about the abuse they had endured that he sent men with them to protect them as they preached and passed out literature! Thus, God was able to use Satan's attack to spread the gospel.

Taylor continued to travel through China, preaching at every opportunity, passing out literature and showing his willingness to suffer for the cause of Christ. In 1865, having been on the mission field for 11 years, the Lord burdened him to begin an organization with the specific intention of reaching the untouched interior of China. He traveled back to England, preaching and writing about the great need to evangelize the millions of lost souls in China. He also began to plead with God to provide the workers he needed to undertake such a great endeavor.

A number of people responded to his call and joined him and his wife in China. Some of these later rose up in pride against Hudson and returned to England, spreading malicious lies about him. He refused to retaliate or even defend himself, leaving it in the hands of the Lord.

Hudson continued to pray to the Lord of the harvest

for workers. By the time of his death, 40 years after starting the organization, there were hundreds of missionaries employed by the China Inland Mission. God used Hudson Taylor and his followers to open up the interior of that great country to the message of Christ. Thousands of Chinese became believers. The Boxer Rebellion attempted to stamp out Christianity, but it only flourished all the more.

Although his organization became one of the most effective and renowned missionary undertakings in the world, Mr. Taylor remained "little in his own eyes." Once, a church leader from Scotland commented to him, "You must sometimes be tempted to be proud because of the wonderful way God has used you. I doubt if any man living has had greater honour."

"On the contrary," Hudson replied. "I often think that God must have been looking for someone small enough and weak enough for Him to use, and that He found me." [8]

In 1905, the small man with the heart as big as the country he was called to evangelize went home to be with his Lord.

These three men are not considered to be "giants of the faith" because they possessed excellent organizational abilities, inordinate strength of character, charisma that rallied followers, or any other notable human quality. They were used by God in a great way because they learned the secret of walking humbly with Him, depending upon Him alone, and serving the needs of other people. Not one of them took personal credit for their achievements; they were all quick to give the glory to God alone. In one sense, they were not special people. Their lives simply typified what Christianity should look like in any believer's life.

THE FRIEND OF GOD

The kingdom of God has been established in such a way that each and every person has the right to receive as many of the blessings of God as he desires. "God is no respecter of persons," Peter said, (Acts 10:34) meaning that the door is open to "whosoever will." What fantastic news!

God does have His favorites, though. This is clearly seen in the history of His dealings with certain men: Abraham was called a "friend of God." (James 2:23) Gabriel twice labeled Daniel as a "man of high esteem." (Daniel 10:11, 19) Scriptures say "The LORD used to speak to Moses face to face, just as a man speaks to his friend." (Exodus 33:11) Believe it or not these men weren't chosen arbitrarily; they had made themselves irresistible to God. They chose to humble themselves before Him and were richly rewarded with His dearest friendship. It was much the same with Jesus. Yes, He spoke to the multitudes and sent out the seventy disciples. However, it was the band of twelve who enjoyed His closest fellowship and even more than they, Peter, James, and John.

"Friendship with God is reserved for those who reverence him," David exclaimed. (Psalm 25:14 LB) It is quite clear that the Lord responds to the actions of humans: He draws near to those who humble themselves before Him. How could He turn a deaf ear to the publican, beating his chest in anguish, brokenhearted over his sin? How could the Lord hold back His blessings from a man like Joseph, who remained faithful through the most difficult circumstances? How could the Almighty close His eyes to the plight of Hudson Taylor who refused to retaliate against his antagonists? How could the Lord ignore the prayers of

"Friendship with God is reserved for those who reverence him."

163

George Mueller, who took up the cause of society's little castaways? From beginning to end, Scripture loudly proclaims the answer: God is overwhelmingly attracted to and undertakes for the lowly.

You have completed this book. I want to encourage you to commit yourself to put the practices outlined herein into your daily life. What you do throughout each day is very important. The Almighty notes every kind word or deed, every time you obey Him, and every occasion that you humble yourself with others. Each such act draws you nearer to Him. Not only that but the more you practice doing good, the easier it becomes to continue it as a lifestyle. Perhaps you will never be an apostle Paul or a Billy Graham, but you can still make yourself a friend to God. How He longs for your friendship!

Humble yourself today. Turn to Him with all your heart. Plead for His help and submit to His will. Watch the Lord transform your character from the inside out. As He does, you will find yourself the recipient of His overwhelming blessings.

≈≈≈

"To this one I will look," Jehovah declared, "to him who is humble and contrite of spirit, and who trembles at My word." This is the person who makes himself *Irresistible to God!*

BIBLIOGRAPHY

CHAPTER ONE

1. Augustine, *City of God*, Nicene and Post Nicene Fathers, Philip Schaff, editor. Ages Software, Inc. Rio, WI (www.ageslibrary.com). Used with permission.
2. Jerome, *The Principle Works of St. Jerome*, Nicene and Post Nicene Fathers, *ibid*.
3. John Cassian, The Works of John Cassian, *ibid*.
4. William Gurnall, *The Christian in Complete Armour*, Vol. 1, The Banner of Truth Trust, Carlisle, PA, 1988.
5. Charles Spurgeon, *Spurgeon's Treasury of the New Testament*.
6. *The Pulpit Commentary*, Vol. XXII, I Peter, MacDonald Publishing Co., McClean, VA. p. 229.
7. *ibid*, p. 213.
8. *ibid*, Vol. V, II Kings, p. 105.

CHAPTER TWO

1. C.S. Lewis, *Readings for Meditation and Reflection*, Harper San Francisco, 1992, p79.
2. A. W. Tozer, *God Tells The Man Who Cares*, copyright 1992. Used by permission of Christian Publications, Camp Hill, PA.
3. William Law, *A Serious Call To A Devout And Holy Life*,

Ages Software.

4. A. W. Tozer, *ibid.*

CHAPTER THREE

1. C.S. Lewis, *Readings for Meditation and Reflection*, Harper San Francisco, 1992, p79.
2. Bishop Hooker, quoted in the *Pulpit Commentary*, Vol. V. II Kings 5, p. 105.

CHAPTER FOUR

1. *Life Application Bible*, Tyndale House Pub., Wheaton, IL, 1988.
2. *Pulpit Commentary*, Vol. VII, Esther, p. 70.
3. John Calvin, quoted in *Keil-Delitsch Commentary*, AGES Software.
4. *Keil-Delitsch Commentary, ibid.*
5. *Pulpit Commentary*, Vol. IV, I Samuel, p. 292.
6. *ibid*, p. 266.
7. *Matthew Henry Commentary*, AGES Software.
8. *ibid.*
9. *Pulpit Commentary*, Vol. V, II Kings, p. 94.

CHAPTER FIVE

1. Proverbs 28:25.
2. *Pulpit Commentary*, Vol. XIV, Obadiah, p. 33.

CHAPTER SIX

1. *Pulpit Commentary*, Vol. XIII, Daniel, p. 160.
2. *ibid*, Vol. IX, Proverbs, p. 310.
3. *ibid*, Vol. X, Isaiah, p. 395.
4. *Strong's Dictionary*, Ages Software.
5. C.S. Lewis, *Readings for Meditation and Reflection*, Harper San Francisco, 1992, p. 80.

6. Steve Gallagher, *Fork in the Road*, Pure Life Ministries, 2001.
7. *Pulpit Commentary*, Vol. IX, Proverbs, p. 327.

CHAPTER SEVEN

1. C.H. Spurgeon, *The Spurgeon Sermon Collection*, Vol. 4, p. 167, Ages Software.
2. Charles Wesley, *And Can It Be*; Hymns of Faith and Life, Light and Life Press (Winona Lake, IN) and the Wesley Press (Marion, IN), 1976; p. 273.
3. William Reed Newell, *Years I Spent In Vanity and Pride*; *ibid*, p. 250.
4. George Whitefield, *Pharisee and the Publican*, AGES Software.

CHAPTER EIGHT

1. Watchman Nee, *The Release of the Spirit*, Christian Fellowship Publishers, Richmond, VA, 2000, p. 15, 98.
2. Dr. & Mrs. Howard Taylor, *Hudson Taylor's Spiritual Secret*, Discovery House Pub., Grand Rapids, MI, 1990, p. 262.
3. Watchman Nee, *ibid*, pps. 38-39, 98.
4. *Pulpit Commentary*, Vol. XI, Lamentations, p. 37.

CHAPTER NINE

1. George Ridout, *The Beauty of Holiness*, AGES Software.
2. Albert Barnes, *Notes on the Bible*, AGES Software.
3. Gayle D. Erwin, *The Jesus Style*, Word Pub., Dallas, TX, 1983, p.92.
4. Steve Gallagher, *At the Altar of Sexual Idolatry*, Pure Life Ministries, 2001.
5. William Law, AGES Software.
6. *Matthew Henry Commentary*, AGES Software.

CHAPTER TEN

1. F.B. Meyer, *Topical Encyclopedia of Living Quotations*, Bethany House Pub., Minneapolis, MN, 1982, p. 102.
2. *Pulpit Commentary*, Vol. XXII, I Peter 5, p. 219.
3. *Mountain Movers Magazine*, the Assemblies of God, c. 1987.
4. A.B. Simpson, *The Bethany Parallel Commentary on the New Testament*, Bethany House Publishers, Minneapolis, MN, 1983, p. 215.

Chapter Eleven
1. Ages Software Questions.
2. Albert Barnes, *ibid.*
3. William Law, *ibid.*
4. Gayle D. Erwin, *ibid*, p. 95.

Chapter Twelve
1. William Law, *ibid.*
2. Basil Miller, *William Carey - The Father of Modern Missions*, Bethany House Pub., 1952, pp. 54 and 149.
3. Reese Publications, P.O. Box 5625, Lansing, IL 60438.
4. George Muller, *The Autobiography of George Muller*, Whitaker House Pub., 1984, pp. 208-209.
5. *ibid*, p. 190.
6. J. Wilbur Chapman, *Present Day Parables*, AGES Software.
7. J. Hudson Taylor, *Hudson Taylor*, Bethany House Publishers, Minneapolis, MN, 1937, pp. 21, 68-69, 145.
8. Dr. & Mrs. Howard Taylor; *ibid*, pps. 226-227.

NOTES

NOTES

NOTES

Other Books Available by
PURE LIFE MINISTRIES

IRRESISTIBLE TO GOD — *NEW FROM STEVE GALLAGHER!*

Before a person can come into intimate contact with a Holy God, he must first be purged of the hideous cancer of pride that lurks deep within his heart.

"This book is a road map that shows the arduous but rewarding way out of the pit of pride and into the green pastures of humility. Here is the place of blessing and favor with God."
—Steve Gallagher

Humility is the key that opens the door into the inner regions of intimacy with God. *Irresistible to God* unfolds the mystery that God is indeed drawn to the one who is crushed in spirit, broken by his sin, and meek before the Lord and others.

WHEN HIS SECRET SIN BREAKS YOUR HEART — *KATHY'S NEWEST BOOK!*

What can be more devastating for a wife than to discover her husband has a secret obsession with pornography and other women? Yet, this is what countless Christian wives face every day. Kathy Gallagher has been there; she understands the pain of rejection, the feelings of hopelessness and the questions that plague a hurting wife.

In this collection of letters, Kathy imparts heart-felt encouragement by providing the practical, biblical answers that helped her find healing in the midst of her most trying storm. The 30-day journal offers wives a place to prayerfully reflect and meditate upon Kathy's letters.

AT THE ALTAR OF SEXUAL IDOLATRY — *OUR BESTSELLER!*

Sexual temptation is undeniably the greatest struggle Christian men face. Here's a book that digs deep and has the answers men are looking for—the kind that *actually* work. *Sexual Idolatry* draws back the curtain and exposes how sexual sin corrupts the entire man, something Steve Gallagher understands: having lived in the bondage of it for over twelve years. Help men put an end to the mystery of lust and maximize God's power in their lives with the proven answers that have helped thousands. *Spanish translation available as well. Sexual Idolatry Workbook also available.*

AT THE ALTAR OF SEXUAL IDOLATRY AUDIO BOOK (4 CDS)

Now you can benefit from the piercing truths contained in *Sexual Idolatry* without actually picking up the book. Whether you are on the go, working at your computer or simply relaxing at home, this moderately abridged audio version of our bestseller will impart God's answers as you listen.

Living In Victory

The secret to victorious living is to tap into God's great storehouse of mercy for one's own needs, and then act as a conduit for that power, directing it toward the lives of others. Overcoming habitual sin is important, but real victory occurs when a person becomes a weapon in the hands of a powerful God against the legions of hell. That is Living in Victory!"
—Steve Gallagher

Break Free From the Lusts of This World

Break Free is by far Steve Gallagher's best writing; its strength is his sobering deliverance of the unvarnished truth to a Church rife with sensuality and worldly compromise. In a time when evangelical Christians seem content to be lulled to sleep by the spirit of Antichrist, *Break Free* sounds a clarion wake-up call in an effort to draw the Body of Christ back to the Cross and holy living. Those with itching ears will find no solace here, but sincere believers will experience deep repentance and a fresh encounter with the Living God.

The Walk of Repentance

The Walk of Repentance is a 24-week Bible study for any Christian that desires to be more deeply consecrated to God. Each week of this easy-to-use curriculum has a theme, addressing the everyday challenges believers face one step at a time. Its simplicity is its strength, using only the Word of God—and occasional stories of saints of old—as its content. Experience the times of spiritual refreshing that follow repentance; go deeper in God as you allow His Word to take root in your heart.

VIDEOS

Breaking Free From Habitual Sin

People try all kinds of methods to break sinful habits, but God has only given one answer to habitual sin: Repentance. Find the freedom you seek; allow the Lord to tear down your old way of thinking and loose the chains that bind you.

Overcoming Insecurity

Insecurities… how many of us have felt their paralyzing effects; yet, how few of us recognize them as the blight of pride? Allow the Lord to dismantle those crippling defense mechanisms that keep you from the abundant Christian life.

When the Temple is Defiled

Christian men in sexual sin often need a wake-up call, a message that pins them to the floor in repentance. This sermon, filmed at Zion Bible Institute during a day of prayer and fasting, describes what happens to those who desecrate their inner being with pornography and sexual sin. God's presence was very strong and used this message to spark great repentance.

AUDIO

Breaking Free From the Power of Lust — *OUR MOST POPULAR SERIES!*

The insidious beast of lust can entrap a person to the point of hopeless despair. But the Lord has given answers that work! The biblical revelations imparted in this series will break the power of lust in the believer's heart. (Four Tapes)

PURE LIFE MINISTRIES

Pure Life Ministries helps Christian men achieve lasting freedom from sexual sin. The Apostle Paul said, "Walk in the Spirit and you will not fulfill the lust of the flesh." Since 1986, Pure Life Ministries (PLM) has been discipling men into the holiness and purity of heart that comes from a Spirit-controlled life. At the root, illicit sexual behavior is sin and must be treated with spiritual remedies. Our counseling programs and teaching materials are rooted in the biblical principles that, when applied to the believer's daily life, will lead him out of bondage and into freedom in Christ.

BIBLICAL TEACHING MATERIALS

Pure Life offers a full line of books, audiotapes and videotapes specifically designed to give men the tools they need to live in sexual purity.

RESIDENTIAL CARE

The most intense and involved counseling PLM offers comes through the **Live-in Program** (6-12 months), in Dry Ridge, Kentucky. The godly and sober atmosphere on our 45-acre campus provokes the hunger for God and deep repentance that destroys the hold of sin in men's lives.

HELP AT HOME

The **Overcomers At Home Program** (OCAH) is available for those who cannot come to Kentucky for the Live-In program. This twelve-week counseling program features weekly counseling sessions and many of the same teachings offered in the Live-in Program.

CARE FOR WIVES

Pure Life Ministries also offers help to wives of men in sexual sin. Our wives' counselors have suffered through the trials and storms of such a discovery and can offer a devastated wife a sympathetic ear and the biblical solutions that worked in their lives.

PURE LIFE MINISTRIES

P.O. Box 410 • Dry Ridge • KY • 41035
Office: 859.824.4444 • Orders: 888.293.8714
info@purelifeministries.org
www.purelifeministries.org